THE GOSPEL OF THE HERE AND NOW

The Book of Mark Speaks to Us Today

The winged lion is a traditional Christian symbol for the author of the Gospel of Mark.

THE GOSPEL OF THE HERE AND NOW

The Book of Mark Speaks to Us Today

Gordon M. Hyde

REVIEW AND HERALD PUBLISHING ASSOCIATION
Washington, DC 20039-0555
Hagerstown, MD 21740

This book was
Edited by Gerald Wheeler
Designed by Richard Steadham
Type set: 11/12 Zapf

PRINTED IN U.S.A.

Library of Congress Cataloging in Publication Data

Hyde, Gordon M.
The gospel of the here and now.

1. Bible. N.T. Mark—Criticism, interpretation, etc. 2. Seventh-day Adventists—Doctrines. I. Title.
BS2585.2.H93 1984 226'.306 84-13371

ISBN 0-8280-0247-9

Contents

CHAPTER 1

It Is His Time

Mark writes a brief, crisp Gospel of the life and teachings of Jesus that has in it the hot-off-the-press quality of the right-here and the right-now. His favorite word—"straightway" (from the Greek *eutheōs),* which pops up in verse 10 of Mark's first chapter and appears throughout the whole book—is like an artist's signature or a papermaker's watermark.

It is almost as though Mark were too impatient to record all the lineage of Jesus (covered by Matthew and Luke) or even the fascinating details surrounding His birth and dedication. The author plunges straight in at the beginning of Christ's ministry. The reader gets one blare of trumpets (quoted from Malachi and Isaiah), and then views the mighty but lowly John the Baptist—the promised "voice" (Mark 1:3), the predicted Elias (Elijah, chap. 9:11-13)—bursting through the backdrop of aging Jewish tradition to present himself center stage in the garb and style of one of the ancient prophets. And the multitudes flock out to the Jordan wilderness to see and hear him.

John the Baptist has come right on time as the forerunner, the preparer of the way for Him whose sandals he would feel unworthy, even as a servant, to unloose.

Yet, in the fullest sense, John is not the one the people look for, except as he is the predicted forerunner of the anticipated Messiah. Men and women have awaited Him through long and tragic centuries of prophetic silence. But now it is almost the time! Announcement, recognition, baptism, and wilderness temptation blend in a tumbling kaleidoscope of color and action. And suddenly it is *His* time!

The fellowship of the Godhead has awaited it. (At least it seems as though God knew and suffered in anticipation. See Revelation 13:8.) Now is the time to demonstrate to a patient universe the depth of God's love, the justice and benevolence of His law—the transcript of His character and the foundation of His kingdom. The Promised One will meet the challenge thrown at God's feet by Lucifer.

Announcements of the momentous event had come to some shepherds and visiting wise men. A handful of faithful watchers kept their vigil—some young, like Mary, others advancing in years like Zacharias and Elizabeth. "Now lettest thou thy servant depart in peace," Simeon breathed into the astonished ear of the officiating Temple priest in whose unsuspecting arms rested the Lord of glory. But even these events did not mark His time in the fullest sense. They did give notice to those whose ears were still tuned to heaven that the moment of His presentation to the nation as the Promised One was at hand.

The Christ child had gone home to Nazareth with Joseph and Mary after His first two or three incredible years and again after the revealing twelfth year of His life. Although the sights and sounds of the Jerusalem Temple had spoken to Him of His mission, He had returned to be their obedient and dutiful Son. But now it is His time! It has been almost twenty years since the Temple experience. The forerunner has dared to condemn the chosen people who have, with smug and often malicious expectation, looked for the coming of their kind of a

Promised One.

People began to wonder if this man in the wilderness, girt with skins and living off the sparse products of the dry and brackish slopes, was not the promised "Elijah." He, in turn, claimed to have baptized One whom he introduced as "the Lamb of God." What could that mean—the Lamb of God? To every Jew, only one thing, one Person. Had they not prefigured the Messiah in sacrifice and offering? Who else could take away the "sin of the world?"

Can it be? This is the universal question asked from the hovels of the common people to the governor's resplendent palace. Yes, it can be. For it is His time!

Nothing in the world is more powerful than a Bible prophecy whose time for fulfillment has come. While the patience of God is infinite, His purposes know no haste and no delay. And there seems little doubt that the "time" proclaimed by our Lord as fulfilled (Mark 1:15) was prophetic time drawn from the apocalyptic prophecies of Daniel.

One of the characteristics of apocalyptic is that it portrays in symbolic language and time units the sweep of history—most generally from the prophet's own day to the end of the age, the time of the end, the coming of the kingdom of glory.

We do well to remind ourselves that such a way of understanding apocalyptic was standard with Christ and the apostles, with the Protestant Reformers and their immediate successors, with the worldwide Advent awakening of the early nineteenth century, and with ourselves as the Seventh-day Adventist Church claiming identification with "the remnant" (Rev. 12:17).

From time to time voices within Adventism have challenged the historicist principles of interpretation, including the year-day principle. Some insist that Scripture contains no explicit evidence to support the year-day principle. But recent studies by leading Adventist scholars in the field of Old Testament have presented abundant evidence beyond the classic Adventist references to Numbers 14:34 and Ezekiel 4:6. Such research provides numerous examples of the year-day principle at work within Bible history. Then by induction and deduction, they have shown the principle to be valid down to the latter-day range of human history.[1]

Likewise, the late L. E. Froom has established beyond question, in his four-volume work on *The Prophetic Faith of Our Fathers,*[2] that the historicist system of interpretation was the standard interpretation of the Protestant Reformation. So when we, as Seventh-day Adventists, persist in retaining the historicist principles of prophetic interpretation and see them reflected in Christ's declaration "The time is fulfilled," we are in what has been the mainstream of Protestant interpretation.

So when Mark records Christ's words, "The time is fulfilled" we take them to refer to Daniel 8 and 9, and especially to 9:25, which indicates the time for the appearance of the Messiah—the Anointed One. At the baptism of Jesus by John in the wilderness the Holy Spirit descended upon Christ in dovelike form, anointing Him to the infinitely sacred work for which He had come.[3]

But in one sense every year of human history has been Christ's "time." When He spared Adam and Eve immediate death for their sin—because of the promise of the Seed of the woman, who should come to roll back the impact of the serpent upon the race and to deliver all who would from the power of sin and the prison house of death—it was His time. He has been the Word of God, the divine *Logos,* to cut through the otherwise impenetrable barrier that sin had dropped between God and man. And He was Saviour and Guide to the chosen descendants of Abraham through whose line He would receive the humanity of His nature here.

In a particular sense, ever since John the Baptist

introduced Him as "the Lamb of God" (John 1:29)—which He became in full at Calvary's cross when He died as substitute after living as substitute—it has been *His* time. Since then the world has been under the fullness of the blessings of the New Covenant, foreshadowed in the sacrifices and ceremonies connected with the Old Testament.

It was His time when He cleansed the Jewish Temple and when He wept over Jerusalem, proud capital for His own chosen people, because they knew neither the time nor the Person of their day of opportunity.

And it was His time when He cried out on Calvary's cross, "It is finished"! The task so long prophesied and so much longer foreseen by the Godhead had been accomplished at the time ordained by prophecy. Now the redeemed—men and women, Jews and Gentiles, all nations and races—are one in Christ Jesus if they will believe on Him.

The time is fulfilled! The great consummation of the ages is about to break upon our world. While men find themselves caught up in everything and anything but preparation for eternity, that very eternity is stealing upon them as a thief in the night—upon all but those who watch by working for His appearing.

Does it all seem too impossible, too remote, too unreal? As it was in the days of Noah, so shall the coming of the Son of Man be. The ancient world received its warnings, entreaties, and invitations. God made the way to be saved from destruction by water simple and plain. It was available to all. But only one family believed enough to commit all to God and His revealed will.

Again it is *His* time! The coming King is at the door. The gospel invitation recorded by Mark is about to be withdrawn. Choose this day whom you will serve, and let it be the Lord!

[1] William H. Shea, *Selected Studies on Prophetic Interpretation*. Daniel and Revelation Committee Series (Washington, D.C.: Review and Herald Pub. Assn., 1982), volume 1.

[2] L. E. Froom, *The Prophetic Faith of Our Fathers* (Washington, D.C.: Review and Herald Pub. Assn., 1946-1954).

[3] For relevant studies of Daniel 8, 9, 11, and 12, see A. V. Wallenkampf and W. R. Lesher, eds., *The Sanctuary and the Atonement* (Washington, D.C.: General Conference of Seventh-day Adventists [printed by Review and Herald Pub. Assn.], 1981), chapters 8-11.

CHAPTER 2

Physician From Heaven

When Christ came to our world to live and die for the salvation of men, in all His work He blended a concern for their physical, mental, social, and spiritual needs. A little thought may suggest how remarkable it was. Greek philosophy led many to despise the body as a trap or prison house for man's immortal soul. What happened to the physical body was really of little importance. The Jews of Christ's day took a different but equally dangerous position. They regarded health or sickness as indicating blessing or guilt. To them anyone sick or handicapped was clearly a sinner. Poverty, illness, or physical deformity revealed the frown of God. Somebody close to the problem must have been a great sinner—either the victim or his ancestors. The sight of a blind man led Christ's disciples to ask, "Who sinned?" (see John 9:1-3).

Added to that pain was the fact that the enemy of man and God had interjected himself so profoundly into the lives of men and women in Christ's day that demons actually possessed them. We have already caught a couple of disturbing hints from Mark's fast-moving story of Christ's opening ministry—signals that associated sickness, poverty, and other calamities with such possession (Mark 1:23-28, 32-34).

We pick up the same suggestion again in Mark 3:11, 12, which gives a general description of the behavior shown toward Christ by those possessed of "unclean spirits." Such entities seemed almost eager to reveal Christ's identity as the "Son of God" as their helpless victims "fell down before him." But it was not an act of worship or devotion. On the contrary, Christ ordered them to desist from making Him known. He showed no interest in their serving as His publicity agents, especially on their terms.

Might we learn from this example that it is never to the advantage of God's cause for believers to be in close touch or have dealings with evil spirits or to permit them any active association with the church? They are *never* seeking to do God or man a helpful service. In the situation described in Mark 3:11, 12 they doubtless played on the inaccurate Jewish expectations of what the Messiah would be like and what would be the nature and purpose of His kingdom. To proclaim Him "the Son of God" at this early stage of ministry could have brought against Christ the kind of prejudice that ultimately led to a charge of blasphemy (chap. 14:53-64).

A young woman attended a series of Adventist evangelistic services in Plymouth, England. Taking Bible studies, she showed great promise of adding strength to the local congregation. She even went to Sabbath services and appeared to be accepting truth step by step. But as she came into closer fellowship with the young people of the church, and as the study of the state of the dead went along, she began to give little signals of possible association with a familiar spirit. When in time she turned away from Adventism, someone asked her why she had come to the meeting in the first place. The woman claimed then that her demon counselor had advised her to do it for "she would learn much truth."

The pastor urged her to request that the church make intercessory prayer for her deliverance from the sinister influence. But she declined. Her entity had trapped her by suggesting, "Work with me for a year in a reforming of art and worship, then make your choice whether to go farther." Eventually she went deeper into spiritualism. Fortunately she did not seem to influence anyone else among the young people to join her in her devotion to the evil one whom she first took to be an agent of heaven rather than of hell.

When Jesus sent the twelve apostles on their missionary journeys, He gave them "authority over the unclean spirits" (chap. 6:7, R.S.V.). One assumes the commission and power included Judas the betrayer. Scripture provides no evidence that Jesus treated him differently from the others in this respect. It may therefore say something to us about His longsuffering attitude with Judas. Also it might suggest that some Christians today may make a name for themselves in apparent healing, exorcism, and other miracles. But it does not mean that their success proves the validity of their relationship to the Lord or the accuracy of their teachings.

The General Conference set up a carefully selected study commission on the topic of demon possession. After much reading, interviewing, and listening, they reached rather clear-cut conclusions and made recommendations.

They did not find in the work of Christ or the apostles anything matching the confrontational aspects that some seem to indulge in. Although it is true that Christ pointed to prayer and fasting as weapons of spiritual warfare, He made no suggestion at the foot of the Mount of Transfiguration that His followers should participate in all-night battles with multiple demons (Matt. 17:1-21). When the Lord or the apostles cast out demons it was with a simple word of command in the power and name of the Lord Himself (Mark 3:13-15; Luke 10:17-20). (Presumably, on their missionary journeys-in-training, the apostles followed their Master's procedure.)

The committee's report goes on to discourage the dialoguing with demons that seems to be a characteristic of this current practice. After evaluating pertinent scriptures and statements from Ellen G. White, the document concluded it could not encourage such activities. Some practioners exhaust themselves in all-night battles with demons, and soon such activity consumes their lives. God's people have not received this kind of end-time commission.[1]

But Mark has more to tell us than just of Christ or His disciples casting out demons. We shall look at three specific incidents of healing that give no hint of direct demon possession: the healing of a leper; the dramatic scene leading to the healing of a paralytic (which brings out some key questions about the relationship of sickness and sin); and a healing on the Sabbath.

The events raise an interesting and vital question: Did Jesus heal by power that was His as God, or was He dependent (as were His followers) upon divine power exhibited through Him in answer to His faith?

While not minimizing the healing of the leper or of the man with a withered hand, may we concentrate upon the healing of the paralytic as we seek answers to our questions? For in the latter we have the Lord openly and directly forgiving a man his sins. Holding in abeyance the question of whether He did so in His own divine power or through the Father's ministered by the Holy Spirit, we have clear evidence that Christ's accusers chose to believe that He took to Himself divine prerogatives. They charge him with being a blasphemer—a crime punishable by death (Mark 2:1-12).

This issue thrusts us into what theology refers to as the *kenosis*—the degree to which our Lord laid aside, or abandoned, or denied, or was dispossessed of His divine rights and powers when He also became a man. Did Christ forgive the sins of the paralytic as God or as an agent of God? How much of His deity was laid aside, abandoned, or taken from Him as part of the price of becoming the God-man in the *kenosis?*

When Christ put the unspoken challenge in the minds of the Jewish religious leaders into words, He said that He would show them that the Son of man had power (*exousia*—authority) on earth to forgive sins (the prerogative of God). He would heal the man, and then they would know that He could do the other as well.

But have we answered the question yet? Was His *exousia* borrowed—entrusted to Him by the Father through the power of angels?

It happens that an able Adventist scholar has recently submitted a doctoral dissertation to the University of Stellenbosch in South Africa. (There are tentative plans for its publication in the Andrews University Dissertation Series.) The author, Professor Eric Claude Webster, who has served as head of the theology department at Helderburg College at Somerset West, investigates four Adventist writers on Christology, including Ellen G. White.

He finds her speaking 125 times of Christ clothing or veiling His divinity with humanity. On the other hand he notes only one occasion where she speaks of His laying aside of His divinity. The proportion of statements and the high concept of Christ's divinity during His incarnation leave little basis for thinking that Christ was shorn of His divinity. It becomes a question then as to how he used His divinity, if indeed He did.

(Let us pause to recognize the great element of mystery present in Christ's incarnation. With that recognition should come a certain hesitance on our part in being dogmatic about the many aspects of the divine-human combination that was the person, Jesus the Christ.)

A dozen or more statements in *The Desire of Ages*

speak of Christ's divinity flashing through His humanity. On such occasions men were helpless before Him. Without doubt our Lord had the power when here to lay His tormentors in the dust by revealing His divinity. So much so that part of His great and persistent struggle and temptation came over His holding His position as man—not using His potential advantage over us in His conflict with sin and the devil.

One of the repeated evidences of Christ's divinity, to which Ellen White points, lay in His power to read men's minds, motives, and futures. And in the incident with the paralytic, according to Mark's account, He must have recognized His accusers' inward questioning of His right to forgive a man's sins. They understood such a prerogative to be God's alone.

While we do not want to overstrain Mark's account of the healing of the paralytic by drawing finer points of distinction than the details warrant, we do note that Scripture does not present anyone but Christ as forgiving a person's sins. God is appealed to for forgiveness (Dan. 9:19; Amos 7:2); Christ is presented as the agent of forgiveness (1 John 2:1, 2) and as the intercessor with the Father in behalf of sinners (Luke 23:34).

The ministry of reconciliation (2 Cor. 5:18) carried by the apostles into the world of their day (Col. 1:23) went forth in the name of Christ. Whether the need was healing, forgiveness, or the expulsion of demons, Christ's followers invoked His name (1 John 2:12 and numerous references in Acts and in the Epistles).

Thus there seems little question that our Lord exercised His own divine authority in forgiving the sins of the paralytic. Interestingly we have no record that the man asked for forgiveness. Again Christ could have been using His divine power to read the victim's mind and the past history of his disease. In any case, to demonstrate His authority the Lord rebuked the disease as He had relieved the burden of sins (Mark 2:8-11).

We apparently need to exercise care and caution in citing an Ellen White statement that Christ performed His miracles through angel ministry.[2] The same source speaks of their being wrought by God's power,[3] Christ's own authority,[4] and Christ's word.[5] Is it not encouraging that all agencies of heaven work in concert for our salvation? And miracles are not an end in themselves. The greatest one of all is that of sinful human nature's being daily transformed by His love and power into the divine likeness.

Ellen White wrote in the January 7, 1890, *Review and Herald,* "The world's Redeemer was equal with God. His authority was as the authority of God. He declared that He had no existence separate from the Father. The authority by which He spoke, and wrought miracles, was expressly His own, yet He assures us that He and the Father are one."

The power lay both in His divine Person and in His great dependence upon His Father and the agency of angel messengers. The authority was His by divine right. None could take it away. He would eventually confront us with the same kind of antithesis at His resurrection. By whose power was He raised? Or did He raise Himself?

---

[1] The General Conference report may be requested from the Biblical Research Institute, 6840 Eastern Avenue NW., Washington, D.C. 20012, U.S.A. Ask for "Spiritual Warfare," May, 1983.

[2] *The Desire of Ages,* p. 143.

[3] *Ibid.*

[4] *The Seventh-day Adventist Bible Commentary,* Ellen G. White Comments, on John 14:9-11, p. 1142.

[5] *The Desire of Ages,* p. 390.

CHAPTER 3

The Lord's Own Family

In Bible times my mother would have been eulogized and men would have stood to their feet in the marketplace when my father passed by. After all, Yahweh obviously favored my parents. They had six boys and six girls.

My father was a German—Johannes Heide—living in London during World War I, and my mother was English—Elizabeth Griggs. They lived on one corner of a side street up over a shop. My German dad had to show his papers periodically at the police station on the other corner.

Born June, 1919, I may have been a celebration that the armistice had been signed. And the family got to move into a housing estate. With the threat of deportation eased, my German father and English mother probably figured they could spend the rest of their days together.

If the national differences were not potential trouble enough, my Adventist father was also a baker. When I came along, I was number thirteen, and the males dominated in our family for a long time. I, the last following a gap of five and a half years, made the baker's dozenth!

Besides being a German in prewar London, my father had to face such questions as "Why do you close your shop on Saturday? Don't you know it is a baker's best day?"

As the youngest I only heard about these things. We had lost our last shop before I came—over the Sabbath. Dad had then gone to Battle Creek for a year and a half and left an unemployed woman in England. How she survived I have never inquired and have no idea. Dad had gone to study health foods under the Kelloggs and planned to bring the secrets back to England to help set up a food factory there.

I don't know the details. Some chapters of our family story my Mum never wanted to talk about. Perhaps they were too painful for her. But she was loyal to her husband. She knew he loved her dearly even though sometimes it seemed to be in funny, trying ways. Not until long after his death did she ever mention such things to me.

My brothers and sisters often found themselves sparring verbally. And you had to be quick and sometimes a bit self-confident to hold your own, a capacity that seemed to cling to us all for the rest of our days.

The older boys had been in the army (World War I), gone to college briefly, then went into the ministry at home or the mission fields abroad: Sierra Leone, Gold Coast (Ghana), Nigeria, Kenya, Tanganyika (Tanzania)—names with mystique. Others were good British ones: Belfast, Manchester, South Wales (Cardiff), Brighton and Hove, Walthamstowe, and Guildford. Places of triumphs and griefs—but all for the Lord and His cause. In our house as long as I can remember we carried them to God in prayer.

And what does this have to do with our Lord and *His* own family? There are parallels. It seems evident that He was a Child of a second wife. On top of that, the village whispered nasty suggestions about some events that had happened. When engaged to Joseph, a carpenter of Nazareth, she was "found with child" (Matt. 1:18). Whether friend or foe, people could ask only one question at that point: Who is the father?

Do you know what it is like to belong to a family where someone or something is different from the normal? Perhaps a child is born deformed or disfigured. Maybe he is the first boy in a school of 200 to wear glasses. Or perhaps he is the only one to observe the Sabbath. He has to leave early on Friday afternoon in order to be out of school before sundown, spoiling a week's perfect attendance for his class and robbing them of one half hour extra recess. Do you know how that loneliness feels? (Sometimes the classmates were more fair and forgiving than the teachers.)

Perhaps he does not fight like most boys and becomes a pillow for the bigger fellows to toss around the room. Or, they bounce him high from a blanket, and someone in the circle lets go when his body comes down.

There is nothing more cruel among birds, beasts, or man, than the treatment suffered by one who deviates from the norm—who is "different" in whatever way.

Joseph, betrothed to Mary, must have been a wonderfully God-fearing man. In an age when a woman had security only in a father or a husband, he thought to be kind to her even when evidence suggested she had been unfaithful. She was pregnant, yet unmarried. And he knew he had not touched her virginity. What should he do with her? Take her to the city fathers at the gate and let them decide? He might have seen enough of that in other cases. If he genuinely loved Mary, and she had pledged herself to him, he was not out to destroy her, not out to humiliate her, or even to leave her to the uncertainties of her situation. Instead he would find a place of retreat and refuge for her until he could decide what would be best for her. Such gentleness in Joseph the carpenter made him great!

Then heaven intervened to explain to Joseph his betrothed's pregnant condition and to give him confidence in her loyalty to him and to her God. But such supernatural conditions and events were not enough to seal the mouths of evil minds. The parentage of our Lord was a frequent target of malicious gossip all His life and even of official innuendo during His ministry. The Lord knew the agony of every illegitimate child, except that His birth was actually free of any taint.

Christ also knew the price of living in a town that had a poor reputation. Humans are so quick to generalize, to categorize, to pick on minorities, the handicapped, the "different" of whatever variety. "Can there any good thing come out of Nazareth?" was the assessment of Christ's hometown, the place where He grew up (John 1:46). Perhaps it was a proverb in Israel. Even a good and devout man, like Nathanael, could ask the barbed question.

But if our Lord's family and neighborhood were typical, it would be as a child and a youth that He would suffer the greatest indignities and hazing. If we rightly understand that the children of Joseph were by a first wife, then they were both older than Jesus and were stepbrothers and stepsisters. They would not relish the stigma brought on the family by the questionable birth of the child of the new woman in the home. Typically the new wife could have encountered resentment just for taking the place of the first wife and the affections of the father, Joseph.

And if the older children were not religiously devout, they could both reject Joseph's account of the angel intervention in behalf of Mary and be prepared to believe the town scuttlebutt on Jesus' birth. Furthermore, if, as it seems, Joseph had died by the time Jesus was in His twenties, then both He and Mary could feel the keen edge of family rejection.

But it was the difference in the ways and words of Jesus that made Him the target of the malice of older brothers and sisters and of the neighborhood youth. It is not what we *profess* that makes us stand out in a crowd.

Rather it is the way we *live,* the kind of persons we actually are on a daily basis.

Picture a child born without taint of sin and who never does anything unkind or selfish or dirty or rude. A child who takes the part of the downtrodden, the poor, the hungry, the despised outcasts of society. Can you imagine the intolerance that would be heaped upon such a Person—the efforts to change Him (so that He would not show up the rest so much)—and the rejection and bitter condemnation of Him when He would not yield? That was our Lord.

When it suited their purposes, the older children in the family would inveigle Mary into doubting Him, fretting about Him, seeking to make Him conform. Mark speaks of this in his Gospel (chap. 3:31-35). And the rabbis were ever in the wings, seeking to corral this Nonconformist!

Did you ever get called on the carpet because of the reports of older brothers or sisters to your parents? It seems likely Jesus did. In Mark 3:20, 21 some of Christ's friends tried to remonstrate with Him for spending His strength on the multitudes—so much so that He was not eating regularly. They wanted to take Him forcibly away from the public eye and get Him straightened around.

The religious leaders among the Jews chipped in with their special wisdom when they came down from Jerusalem. They said Christ was so different, so odd, so unbalanced, that He was under the control of the prince of the devils. Even His miracles they attributed to demon power. That's how far the human mind can be twisted when it determines not to believe what it sees!

It may have been as a result of such efforts that Mary condescended to join Joseph's children in their search for Jesus and attempt to bring Him under their control, to force Him home were they could deal with Him.

Every younger child in a family can remember such

episodes. They are not easy to take. But our Lord made a vital spiritual statement about His supposed devil possession and about the makeup of His family. His world-renowned "house divided" illustration (adopted by Lincoln in his fight against slavery) nullified the accusation about His familiarity with devils. And His inquiry as to who really were His mother and His brethren showed the superiority of the relationships of our spiritual family to our physical one.

"Who is my mother, or my brethren?" was the crucial question Jesus asked. And we can repeat it after Him. Who really is my mother, who really are my brothers and sisters? Happy is he who finds his earthly family at the heart of his spiritual one. No law of psychology or of spirituality will deny such a delightful possibility. And we want to hasten to point to Mary's devotion to her mysterious Son. To Golgotha she followed Him and He saw her there, swaying and fainting with grief. He dearly loved her. It had only been His love for her that led Him to keep her from intervening between Him and the heavenly Father when she could not understand all His ways.

At 12 years of age He had already understood that and virtually demanded that she and Joseph ever recognize the priority of the divine relationship. (And yet He went home with them in filial obedience for another eighteen years.)

Is His will so much yours that it seems like your own? Then you are a member of His intimate family. You are more than His earthly mother, brother, or sister except as they, too, trusted Him for righteousness imputed and yielded to His Spirit for righteousness imparted. Perhaps the writer of the Epistle of James (along with Mary and Joseph) was at least one member of our Lord's human family who also found salvation in Him.

Today we meet increasing numbers of church members who have met grief in home and family. So many wounded and scarred lives! So much rejection, heartache, suffering, helplessness, and impoverishment! The taking of sides, the vying for loyalty. The pitting of child by one parent against the other in the throes of all that makes up a divorce—a bewildered and pained child who loves them both. Heaven aches for the grief and misery of it all.

Jesus understands such stresses, jealousies, and fears from His own family on earth. Press close to His spiritual family—your mothers and fathers, brothers and sisters in Christ, His church! Never let Him or them go. And church family, watch out for all your children!

CHAPTER 4

Master of All Fears

When anyone admits that he is afraid of something—of anything—he lays himself open for he knows not what. He is at least likely to have a second fear of being despised, ridiculed, or rejected.

As a child, I was terrorized by anything big or tall or that made a deafening noise. Tall chimney stacks, water towers, multistoried buildings, steam engines, ship's sirens, all overwhelmed me with fear. For a long time I just knew that airplanes ran on wires, and when they came low, something dreadful had gone wrong. But the most paralyzing fear of all was of being in unprotected high places.

I wrestled for years with Christ's interest in or concern for such small-boy fears. Phobias, they call them. But giving them a technical name doesn't help. And a boy ain't sposed t' be skeered o' nuffin! But he is. Especially if he was sick a lot or weakened by disease as a child. Does Jesus care?

What if we add the supernatural and unaccountable to the natural and accountable sources of fear? Does God have anything for us there? What of the fear of death or of the torture of a righteous person?

Mark's Gospel has a number of interesting and helpful things to say to us about our fears. This chapter will examine three areas: (1) the fear of elemental powers—storms, wind, waves, water, drowning; (2) the fear of supernatural forces devoted to evil purposes; and (3) the fear of sickness, pain, suffering, and death.

For those who have crossed the oceans girdling our world, the knowledge that the "sea" on which Christ and His disciples came face to face with disaster was less than ten miles wide makes it seem insignificant and utterly unreal. (At the same time, the boredom of our transoceanic jet flights may be robbing the present generation of any realistic concept of the vastness of our oceans.) But here was Jesus in desperate danger—according to the able seamen He had on board—on a little patch of water, a fresh water lake thirteen miles long and eight miles wide at its greatest breadth.

But that lake had other distinctive characteristics, some of which had a bearing on the ferociousness and unpredictable nature of the storms that terrified seasoned fishermen. The sea lies about 696 feet below the level of the Great Sea (or Mediterranean) and its greatest depth reaches over 150 feet. The low elevation of the surface gives a semitropical climate to the area and creates variations of temperature and air pressure that aggravated the suddenness of developing storms. High hills surround the lake except where the Jordan River enters and leaves it. Developing winds can whistle through the gaps and valleys between and among the hills, which almost act like air ducts, to whip the surface of the lake into an almost instantaneous frenzy.

Following a full day of teaching multitudes that crowded Him against the lapping waters of the lake, our Lord proposed a change of program. He would like to cross to the other side of the lake—probably a west-to-east crossing. For some of the disciples who had spent their lives fishing for the score or more varieties of fish in the lake, such a trip was routine. The Lord had used a fishing boat for His pulpit all day (Mark 4:1). So they just pushed off after dispersing the crowd, but other boats joined them to see where the Master would go next (verse 36).

The picture of Christ sleeping and the exhaustion of the expert seamen may suggest the passage of evening hours—a short twilight, and the intensified darkness brought on by the storm. Perhaps Jesus rested on the leather pillow on which the oarsman sat to steer the vessel.

The waves beat into the boat as though it had no sides. Were the landlubbers among the disciples bailing, or were they too seasick? Now if the brilliance of lightning against darkness, the crash of thunder, and the banshee shriek of wind in rigging were not enough to waken our Lord, we have the fact that the boat is full of water and it seems unlikely that it would not have sloshed over the Saviour's sleeping, prostrate form.

Do good people—believing, dedicated individuals—ever get angry at God? There seems to be some hint of anger in the cry, "Master, carest thou not that we perish?" (verse 38). Perhaps they had decided that He had no concern about whether *He* perished. He could go back to His Father. But they? And who was He really? Did they really really know yet?

Lloyd J. Ogilvie sees a connection between the evening's activities and Christ's teaching through the day. The parable of the sower, the seed, and the soils was having its real application in the disciples themselves. What kind of hearers of the Word of God were they? The way they reacted when Christ finally stilled the waves makes one question if their faith had moved far above the level of superstition.[1]

But let's update the scene a moment. Our world has lots of treacherous waters. Places where the crew at times has to lash down everything movable, where the water slaps and seethes in the scuppers, when a combined pitch and roll over a mountainous crest leaves the passenger's stomach suspended in space followed by the horrible sinking feeling at the bottom of the drop. And it can go on and on all night. Afraid? Who isn't? Experience tells the captain that his vessel has weathered all this before. But that is not always enough. The fatal condition is one that exceeds in some way all past experiences that we have survived.

Your airline captain comes on with that voice that is just too calm: "Ladies and gentlemen, we have just lost oil pressure in our two starboard engines and have had to shut them down. We are X kilometers from the nearest airport that can handle this aircraft. Please keep calm. Keep your seat belts securely fastened, and we will keep you informed of our progress. We are trying to raise a signal from the airport now."

How could Jesus lie there in that pitching, rolling, waterlogged little fishing boat and sleep? Of course it is amazing what a person can sleep through when he is exhausted or when he is young and sinks swiftly into what some psychologists call the fourth level of sleep. As children, some of us have slept through storms that took a tent or almost half a house away. Was that the case with Jesus? Or did He lie there in the calm certainty that as Master of ocean, earth, fire, and air, He was immune? Big questions, for which we will not have complete answers until the Lord gives them in person.

In any case, whatever gave Him the ability to sleep presumably gave Him the authority to say to the storm, "Peace, be still" (verse 39). What power Jesus used then was governed, most probably, according to what He gave up, or laid aside, when He became the Son of man. We can never doubt that He made an infinite sacrifice of Himself to become our Substitute and Surety. But He was still God and may have called upon His divine prerogatives, except as it gave Him some advantage in the conflict with temptation or allowed Him to avoid suffering and inconvenience.

The selfishness of the human heart—as well as occasional heroics of unselfishness—shows up in a crisis. Perhaps the disciples were not yet fully convinced that Jesus was indeed God. They said, " 'Teacher, don't you care if we drown?' " Did they include Him in the "we"? Did they think that He was tempting Providence or that He had a death wish? But after He had said to the waves, " 'Quiet! Be still!' " He asked the disciples, " 'Why are you so afraid? Do you still have no faith?' " (verses 38-40, N.I.V.). What is the connection between fear and faith? Perhaps human fear during terrible danger is natural and to be expected. But at least faith can take the paralyzing, berserk element out of it.

What is perhaps the more remarkable (to us, at least) is the disciples' reaction when the storm calmed. "They were terrified and asked each other, 'Who is this? Even the wind and the waves obey Him!' " (verse 41, N.I.V.). How could men, solidly assured of the full and real identity of the Omnipotent One, respond in such a way? It hardly seems possible. Should it not then give us a deeper view of the mercy and patience of our Lord with the blindness and unbelief of His closest followers? And maybe we could afford to be equally as accepting toward our fellow believers—both within or without our own special ranks—when they do not understand everything about the mysterious combination of the divine and the human in our Lord.

Their reaction to the stilling of the tempest puts them close to the superstitious. Mark's account gives the impression that Christ's control of the storm terrified them more than the dangerous storm itself. Awe, reverence, worship—these could rightfully result from Christ's power over the storm. But terror?

Fear, faith, power, terror—what a strange sequence of emotions and actions. But what a comfort to have illustrated for us that a lack of faith, even while in the personal presence of the Saviour, does not lead Him to reject us. He does not abandon us when our paralyzing fear overwhelms our faith in His power to save. Jesus often rescued His unbelieving, distrusting disciples, even toward the close of their three years of intensive instruction and training.

Such gentle condescension on the part of the Creator-Sovereign of the universe reminds us of the counsel that when we are too sick to pray, we can still trust, can still rest in His care. Our trusting is in itself a prayer of great eloquence, to which He responds with an infinitude of power. "Often your mind may be clouded because of pain. Then do not try to think. You know that Jesus loves you. He understands your weakness. You may do His will by simply resting in His arms."[2]

Some wonder whether Jesus was kept from harm in the storm because, as God, He could not be harmed, or whether heaven protected Him in response to His continual manifestation of faith and obedience in and to His Father. Likewise, whether in stilling the storm He exercised His power as Lord of the oceans and skies or received it in response to His faith-relationship with His Father. In a way, it does not matter how—only that the power was available and manifested then and can be now in response to our need and our faith in our Lord. But as suggested earlier, the final answer resides in what Jesus actually gave up or laid to one side when He carried out the covenant to become our divine-human Saviour.

The Desire of Ages indicates clearly at this point in Christ's experience that "it was *not* as the 'Master of earth and sea and sky'" that Jesus rested calmly in the seemingly doomed boat.[3] One would gather, therefore, that He calmed the angry winds and waves through His dependence on the Father. It would harmonize with His words "I can of mine own self do nothing" (John 5:30). Yet, as the already-mentioned doctoral dissertation by Eric C. Webster points out, in some respects Christ's divinity galvanized His humanity—but not for His personal comfort or safety, or to help Him resist temptation.

We don't know how the terrorized disciples nursed their superstitious fears about the kind of Man who could command wind and waves. But if they were still mulling them over when the familiar grating of keel on beach led them through the routine of disembarking and securing their boat, they soon had other demands upon their attention. (If we wonder why the Lord would put His disciples through such a sequence of trials of their faith, we could always remind ourselves that they were in a school. Their course was intense and compressed. Think of how little time Jesus had with His followers before He would entrust the future of His cause to their hands.)

Faced with a threat more frightening than that of the storm at sea, they raced for the boat that had been the seat of all their recent troubles. And they left their Lord and Master alone to face a demon-possessed individual, just as ultimately they would forsake Him at the approach of the ragtag mob in the Garden of Gethsemane.

Thus we find ourselves thrust into the heart of another of Mark's lightning sketches of open conflict between Christ and the evil spirits that contested His every step in service to humankind. If He had come to reveal the Father to the human family, Satan would summon every resource at his disposal to hinder, thwart, or mar that portrayal.

Of the six specific instances of demon possession recorded in the Gospels, Mark mentions five, including this most dramatic incident of them all. Picture the Master of all our fears calmly awaiting the approach of a man who had terrorized the district of Gadara by his appearance, his unearthly shrieks, and his ability to overpower strong men sent to bind him.

It is the same Son of man who had continued sleeping through the devastating storm of the past night. Whereas the fishermen among the disciples had wrestled with the storm—to the point of forgetting their Lord was among them—now they have forgotten the weapons He had given them for coping with the hideous and tormented specimen of humanity who had come rushing down from the tombs (Mark 3:13-15). As the demoniac draws near he assumes an attitude of worship. But the disciples have apparently forgotten the recent miracle. Finally it must dawn upon them that the Saviour is not among them, that He is dealing with the demoniac (or two of them, as Matthew records).[4]

In a previous chapter we alluded to the rise of exorcism within the ranks of the Seventh-day Adventist Church. It draws some of its Biblical support from this particular event in Christ's ministry. And without any desire or intent to judge the motives or to anticipate the practical fruitage of this activity, we would wish to make several observations.

That the demon in one or both of the demoniacs declared his name to be Legion, "for we are many" (chap. 5:9), is not an adequate basis for asserting the general principle that demon possession is usually multiple. It does not mean that in modern instances of possession scores of demons control each person.

The fact that in this instance a brief interchange took place between the demons and Christ (initiated, evidently, by the former in recognition of Christ's person and power), and even that demons seemed eager to identify the Christ on other occasions, does not provide enough basis to form a principle. If confrontation and identification of the demons were part of a divinely conceived and authorized formulary for exorcism, then one would expect the Lord Himself to provide such instruction to His disciples when He gave them power to cast out spirits. Scripture should have recorded their practice of it for the guidance of the church through the Christian Era.

To justify extended questioning of supposed multiple demons in our day on the basis of the Gadara experience hardly demonstrates "rightly dividing the word of truth" (2 Tim. 2:15). Anyone who initiates conversation with professed demons risks the danger of having them intrude into his own mind and life.

If you are a rich and powerful man, a leader in your community, a high officer in the church, and your little girl hovers at the point of death, you are desperate—especially in the days of Jesus, when medical knowledge was in its infancy. And if you are a lonely woman who has been sick twelve years and you have spent all your money on doctors to no avail, you are also desperate and filled with crippling fear. At that point, money is no longer the key to what you need most. Death is the great leveler. (See Mark 5:21-43 for the two stories.)

Now, we live in a different age and circumstances than faced the daughter of Jairus or the nameless woman who had been sick twelve years. Most of us could probably obtain medical help to meet our needs. But it could help ease the tensions that exist today even in the church between the well-to-do and the less fortunate if both could know that God cares about the fears of each. He loves the one as well as the other. Christ came to give His life for the salvation of the one equally with the other.

Was the woman now a widow? Had she been the loving center of a happily situated family? What had happened to them? Could her problem have carried a burden of guilt? We do not know. Doubtless others considered her as ceremonially unclean, with the added strain that such a stigma would bring.

Jairus, on the other hand, was a family man with at least one daughter. His wife was doubtless living. He had servants—faithful and thoughtful servants. And he doubtless had means and considerable influence and prestige.

It doesn't take a vivid imagination to see these two human beings, distraught with fear—the fear of sickness and death—searching out the Life-giver. In one way it was easy to find Him. Just head for the biggest crowd around. The next problem was to get close enough to gain His attention.

If the woman died before she could have that desired moment in His presence, who would know, who would care? Seemingly she had no human supporters. Would her body end up in a potter's field or in the nearest Gehenna?

Should Jairus' daughter—who was dying when he left home—perish before he could find the Master and divert Him to his house, it would break his heart. Either because he and she had that special something between father and daughter, or perhaps because his religious duties had led him to neglect her and now he would be beaten down with remorse.

There almost seems to be a contest between Jairus and the woman. Which of them would find Him first? To whose need would He more readily respond? All the odds of the social fabric of her day were against the woman. Did our Lord follow them both in their quest? Had He been drawing them both to believe He could quell their fears and meet their needs?

Suddenly Jairus' problem takes a quantum leap. "Your little girl is dead." One of his faithful servants has found him, knowing his master would be somewhere near the Master. In fact, Jairus has already made his need known. But the clogging crowds . . . and Jesus seems not to know how to hurry. So many need His help.

You can just see Jairus' hands flip upward in a gesture of despair. But listen to the words of Jesus, who has overheard the confidential message. Will He say, "Well, that was too bad. I had every intention of coming and helping. But you see the crowds. And you know there was that poor woman." No, that is not the Lord's answer. Never taken by surprise, His work is not haphazard. His heart picks up the beat of everyone's fear. "Be not afraid," He tells Jairus.

But what good is that? Don't be afraid, when the child is dead? It was one thing to believe Christ could have healed her. But now, she is gone—and that is very final. The family immediately begins the mourning rites. The rabbis said that the poorest family must have two flutes and one lamenting woman when the wife died. What would they have at Jairus' house? "Be not afraid, only believe."

The sick woman had believed, and her faith had driven her to use her last ebbing strength to search for the Lord. Should she talk to the Great Healer herself? She had no idea what to say. Suddenly she had seen Him slipping by in the crowd. No time to speak. Almost in a swoon, with the last of her strength, she touched the border of His garment. But something happened—and she knew it immediately. He, the center of all attention, stopped and kept looking right at her. Had she done wrong? Was it discourteous to touch even the garment of the Man? But why did He seem to want to embarrass her by exposing her? Because she must not misinterpret what had happened. It was not magic. Dynamic power flowed from Him to her in response to the act of her faith. The milling, crushing crowd got nothing from its casual brush against His robe.

Because of her testimony, perhaps something new got started. People began to touch "the border of His garment: and as many as touched him were made whole" (chap. 6:56).

When the Lord finally reached Jairus' house, He did

not need directions. The funeral had begun. The people were paid, so there was no sincerity to their wailing. Jesus put the whole lot out. Then He took Peter, James, and John—a special group within the disciples—and the parents and went in to where the family had lovingly laid out the little girl.

When Jesus had said that she was only sleeping, the crowd responded with derisive and unsympathetic laughter. But it affected Him not at all. The Lord always knew what He was doing. Then His words to the little girl suggest that Jesus spoke Aramaic: *Talitha cumi* ("Wake up, little one!")—as her mother might call her any morning.

Be not afraid! Only believe. All things are possible to him that does (chap. 9:23).

---

[1] Lloyd J. Ogilvie, *Life Without Limits, the Message of Mark's Gospel* (Waco, Texas: Word Books, 1975), pp. 82-91.

[2] *The Ministry of Healing*, p. 251.

[3] *The Desire of Ages*, p. 336.

[4] *Ibid.*, pp. 337, 338.

CHAPTER 5

PR Man Murdered

In modern terms John the Baptist would be Jesus' public relations man, an advance man, whose task it was to develop a publicity campaign for the One to whom the nation's attention must be drawn. Indeed, he would work to prepare a climate of opinion and attitude that would make acceptance of the new Leader attractive and desirable. The process of fulfilling his appointed role led to the murder of this public relations man. And that was after serving the greatest Miracleworker the world has ever seen!

Mark is especially brief and typically cryptic on some items. Early in his Gospel he refers to John's preaching, Christ's baptism, and John's arrest. At that same point he introduces the gospel of Christ's preaching (chap. 1:14, 15). He gives no account of John's heartrending question that he sent to Jesus through His disciples. We are dependent on Matthew and Luke for that.

How long had John languished in Herod's dungeon and why? Possibly a year, maybe less. And for daring to apply his specific call for repentance to people in positions of influence, intrigue, and power.

Struggling with his loneliness and seemingly complete abandonment by Christ, John asked for some confirmation of his original confidence in His Messiahship. We may sense also that it rent the heart of the Lord that He should subject His cousin to such a trial. It must have grieved Him that one who had been filled with the Spirit, one led by Him to know and identify "the Lamb of God," should now wrestle with doubt.

Notice that Jesus followed His gentle rebuke included in His answer to John—"'blessed is he who takes no offense at me'" (Matt. 11:6, R.S.V.)—with a divine-human testimony that no man born was greater than John (verses 7-15). But still the hand that quieted raging storms and dominated demons did not lift in defense of John. From our human standpoint, that is one of the most difficult to explain of Jesus' inactions.

Could not God have sent the angels that later brought Peter out of prison, leading him from between the guards to whom he was chained, through multiple heavy doors and further guard units and even the prison gate itself, to aid John? Without question. Could not Christ Himself have conquered physical laws, as He did in walking on water, and have brought John out? Then why didn't He?

John's imprisonment had no legal basis. A sensuous and scheming woman had manipulated a weak king into casting the Baptist into prison.[1] We can understand therefore why John's situation could trouble Christ's own disciples.[2] Judas would particularly see it as political suicide for his schemes for Christ if Jesus did not deliver John or if the Baptist should be killed.[3]

But when John's disciples brought him Christ's enacted answer (whereby His works testified to His mission and His message), the faithful evangelist took no offense at the rebuke. Taking courage over the confirming evidence, he saw again that fulfilled prophecy authenticated the Messiah's mission and was satisfied now to await the outcome of events, whatever they might be. The words John had spoken in the wilderness of Judea—"He must increase, but I must decrease" (John 3:30)—had been the keynote of his life and ministry. Never had they reached such a height of demonstration as in the imprisonment (and later death) measured out to a man of fearless integrity.

When one thinks of the learning privilege extended to the twelve apostles of Jesus, and even to larger groups of His disciples, one could even suggest the Baptist's opportunity to understand everything about the Messiah was quite limited. Compare John's question with that of the apostles and disciples after His resurrection. After His repeated visits to them over a five-week period to assure them of the reality of His resurrection, they still asked Christ if He would *at that time* give back the kingdom to Israel (Acts 1:1-6).

Christ prepared to ascend to His Father permanently, and the disciples wanted to know if He would now, as the Messiah, do what all Jews had been taught by tradition that the Anointed One would do. Would He *now* break the Roman domination and give Israel back its full control of the Land of Promise? In spite of the fact that the apostles were still looking for kingdom-of-glory prophecies to be fulfilled at kingdom-of-grace-preaching time, the Lord was patient, kind, and gracious in His reply.

We do well to remember that John the Baptist grew up with the same tradition in the home and ministry of his father, Zechariah the priest. And not until he saw in the reported works of Christ the fulfillment of the prophetic words of Isaiah—the gospel witness in the Old Testament—was he satisfied. Now he saw more clearly that the spirit that had marked his life and his mission as the advance man for the Messiah was the same one that would characterize even more the life and mission of his Master. If he, John, must suffer unjustly for other men's sins, how would it be with Him in whom there never had been one trace of selfishness?

John the Baptist truly was the forerunner of Jesus. So deeply did he reflect the character of Him who came to be our Servant that Christ could entrust to John the high honor of sharing in His sufferings. For a human being there is no greater honor.

Possibly no Bible character other than the Son of God Himself has left to the Christian Era a greater example of selflessness. No one had a truer estimate of his sinful, selfish human nature, than had John. Finding nothing good in himself to boast about, he would not even bring himself to claim as his right the position of a slave in relationship to his master.

The Baptist was everything that a true PR man for Christ should be. When we recall that Christ claimed for John the Elijah role foretold by Malachi (chap. 4:5, 6) and we consider that there is to be an Elijah people with an Elijah message "before the coming of the great and dreadful day of the Lord," we can scarcely give John too much of our attention. Let us list what he *was,* what he *did,* and what he *taught.* It might give us a clearer picture of the message and mission of the Elijah people awaiting the Second Coming.

What John was

1. A fearless and effective voice in the wilderness.
2. A foreseen and foretold child.
3. A Nazarite, filled with the Spirit.
4. A reformer, an evangelist.
5. A forerunner of the Christ.
6. A fulfillment of Bible prophecy.

What John did

1. He lived a life of separation, consecration, strict temperance, and simplicity.
2. He prayerfully studied God's books of nature, providence, human experience, and revelation.
3. He preached repentance of sin, and restitution to a life of surrender and obedience.
4. He gave a message suited to all classes.
5. He prepared a people for the Messiah-Lord.
6. He watched for the first appearance of his Lord.

7. He baptized in water those who gave evidence of accepting his message of repentance of sin.
8. He gave instruction on what God expected of the penitent believer.
9. He particularly studied Bible (Old Testament) predictive prophecies.
10. He preached penitence (forgiveness, justification) and obedience (laws particularly pertinent to different groups in society).
11. He lived largely as he preached—by faith in Christ.
12. He baptized (not without protesting the necessity of it) the sinless Son of God.
13. He saw the symbol of the Holy Spirit descend upon the Christ.
14. He heard the Father's announcement and benediction.
15. He accepted a band of disciples.
16. He had a special burden for the Jews (his own people), but he also had a message for all.
17. He identified Christ, whose outward appearance would not have identified Him to men.

What John taught

1. That the universal need of repentance rested upon the universally sinful nature of the human race.
2. That the appearance of the Messiah was imminent.
3. That he, John, was unworthy, spiritually, to be Christ's slave-servant.
4. That, nevertheless, God had brought him into existence to prepare the way of the Lord.
5. That he, John, should ready the people to expect Him and to receive Him.
6. That while he baptized with waters of repentance and cleansing, the Coming One would baptize with the Holy Ghost and with fire.

7. That the Promised One was among them (unrecognized because He did not meet Jewish expectations).
8. That the One to whom he pointed was indeed the Lamb of God who had come to take away the sin of the world.
9. That Christ must increase while he (John) must decrease.
10. That he would introduce his disciples to Jesus, that they might follow Him.

Let us raise the question again: If John the Baptist was the Elijah messenger for Christ's first Advent, what can the people called to be the Elijah messengers before the final great and dreadful day of the Lord learn from him? Where shall we start?

- The Lord called him at a particular time foretold in apocalyptic prophecy.
- He was to bear a particular and special message of reformation to the professed people of God and those in contact with them.
- He was to denounce sin wherever it had infiltrated church and nation.
- His life was to demonstrate the principles he taught.
- He gave a message by example of simplicity of lifestyle, temperance in living, and noninvolvement with the world's consuming interest.
- He pointed away from himself to Christ in recognition of his own inadequacy and of Christ's all-sufficiency.
- He called for cleansing of the life through the symbol of water baptism in order that the power of the Holy Spirit might come upon the obedient to transform their nature and endow them with power for witnessing.
- He was free from political ambition and actions based on self-serving policy. Seeking only a servant's place, he even felt unworthy of that.
- His message called men to judgment before the bar of

God.

- His supreme joy was in pointing men—even his own little band of disciples—to Christ, for John had no eternal life to give.
- He lived and died with one unwavering purpose and mission directing his life—that of pointing men to Christ as the sole solution to the sins of the church and the world.
- He was persecuted and vilified for his fearless denunciation of sin wherever it existed.

When the guards came to take his head to a drunken and besotted orgy of high officials—many of whom gave intellectual assent to John's prophetic call and message—they only ushered him into the kingdom of glory, the next thing this faithful soldier of the cross will know.

---

[1] *The Desire of Ages,* p. 214.
[2] *Ibid.,* p. 249.
[3] *Ibid.,* p. 718.

CHAPTER 6

Dogs Under the Table

We once had a dog whose basket we kept under the dining-room table so that there would be less danger of someone stumbling over it and him. The living room was also our family room, since it had the only fireplace used to combat the wet and penetrating cold of the winter's bluster. Occasionally during a meal a heedless and shoeless foot might wander over the top of the dog's basket, perhaps landing on his head or ear. A sudden yelp of protest would follow, perhaps even a nip at the offending foot, producing yells, screams, and a general confusion. But when Christ spoke of dogs under a table, they did not sleep in padded baskets.

The typical dog in Bible times did not get his distemper shots, worm powders, or flea collars. Neither did he get that careful balance and ration of food that gave him an excellent chance of enjoying better health and proportionate longevity than his master. The animal in Christ's day was often an argument in favor of evolution—it was a question of survival, and therefore survival of the fittest (and meanest and quickest) of the pack.

Cities in Christ's day might have had brilliantly planned viaducts and cisterns carved out of solid rock by sheer hard labor, but when it came to sanitary engineering, they left much to be desired.

Nature, however, has her own cleanup crews, who can handle anything. Special varieties of birds, beetles, and bacteria show up only when carrion and garbage are in abundance. And at the head of them all in Bible times were the dogs. They still serve as the sanitary corps in many parts of the world. Ever hungry, never satisfied, they are always ready to compete with vultures, carrion crows, hyenas, and the like. Not completely wild, but far from tame, they live by their wits and by varying degrees of tolerance. And they provided the symbol the Jews had for the peoples of all other nations. When Shakespeare has Shylock accusing Bassanio and his friends of calling the Jew a dog, he was echoing in reverse a Biblical custom.

As I. H. Marshall indicates, " 'dogs' was a well-known term of opprobrium for Gentiles, but it is going against all that we know of Jesus to imagine that He could have voiced this insult."* Then what is He doing suddenly in Syrophoenician country and how has this mother, a Greek, learned that this peasant Jew has any powers that will meet the needs of her little daughter?

Mark is cryptic as usual, but has those little touches of detail that shed light. If he did indeed write more for Gentile than for Jewish believers, his account of Christ's sudden sally into Gentile territory would be of immense interest and encouragement to all non-Jewish readers and particularly the believers in the city of Rome.

The swift journey north and west has particular fascination for us today. Christ has traveled north of Samaria, north of Galilee, and into the territory surrounding the ancient port cities of Tyre and Sidon. He is in the territory that now forms the small country of Lebanon.

Whom did Jesus know up there? Were Jews of the dispersion there, as in most major cities of the eastern Mediterranean regions? Who would open his home to Him as a place of refuge and relaxation? "He entered a house, and would not have anyone know it; yet he could not be hid" (Mark 7:24, R.S.V.). Was the home lent to Him, as the borrowed foal later, or the upper room for the Passover? The latter incidents happened in Jewish territory. Who knew enough about Him to offer such hospitality among the Gentiles?

In another earlier setting Mark mentions people "from about Tyre and Sidon" as part of "a great multitude, hearing all that he did," who came to Jesus by the Sea of Galilee. They were there when He called for a boat to be available to Him "lest they should crush him; for he had healed many" (chap. 3:8, 9, R.S.V.). On this occasion also it seems most likely that He delivered the demon possessed. So here is one specific link by which the woman could have learned of Jesus.

Mark gives us the impression that Jesus had scarcely been shown to His room, had His feet bathed, and laid off His outer garments before the Greek mother knocked at the gate or pulled on the bell rope.

Only those who have had a little one lying in their arms, apparently dead, can know the distraught state of mind of a parent in such a case. The mother speaks to the child with all the pleading of her breaking heart, hoping that it will respond. The father wrings his helpless hands, wracks his wearied brain for some clue, some gleam of light, of help, of inspiration. He takes the child from the mother, hugs it to his bosom, gazes down into those dull and unresponsive eyes, and cries out to God unashamedly in his deperation: "Oh, God, help us! Oh, God, save our baby!"

We don't know the age of this "little daughter." Being a little girl was not in her favor. Her father does not appear in the story. Was he unable to bring himself to approach this Jewish prophet? Was he a Jew or a Greek? Was he already dead? We don't know. But according to Matthew the woman "came out and cried, 'Have mercy on me, O Lord, Son of David.'" How did she know so much? How did she know what to call Him? Then she told of the child's problem.

"But he did not answer her a word." Was He so tired that He was just a little annoyed to have His peace disturbed? It almost seems that the disciples at least had this attitude. They begged the Lord to send her away, " 'for she is crying after us' " (Matt. 15:21-23, R.S.V.).

Do you know what it is like to have mothers or their children swarming around you, begging for a coin or a morsel? And you either have none, or have offered all you had, or just don't intend to give? How are you going to get rid of them? Call for a policeman to drive them off?

And now comes the great lesson for the disciples and for all people as to Christ's attitude toward other nations and races—a lesson all have been so slow to learn and with which we all still struggle. He tells her that He had been sent only to the " 'lost sheep of the house of Israel' " (verse 24, R.S.V.). Surely that should silence her. She is, after all a Greek, a Syrophoenician, a heathen woman. Even she should understand that. Did the disciples add, "That's right, woman. Begone! Don't bother our Master anymore. Go home!"?

But maternal love motivates her. And Christ Himself may be drawing this woman to Himself, to make known her need. She does not give up easily, is not through yet. Kneeling before the Lord, she *begs* Him, " 'Lord, help me' " (verse 25, R.S.V.).

The final test and development of her faith in Christ as Lord follows. He who pronounced woes on any who would cause one of God's little ones to stumble, now tells her that it is not right to take bread from the children at their father's table and throw it to the dogs! (And what a snarling and scrapping there would be over every morsel!) But the Lord who had come to give His life for this woman may have given a little help to her faith when He said—as Mark records—" 'Let the children first be fed, for it is not right to take the children's bread and throw it to the dogs' " (chap. 7:27, R.S.V.).

Did the Greek mother pick up a tone in His voice, an expression in those eyes that told her the Lord was only drawing out her faith? No matter. In holy boldness, and yet with meek reverence, she responds, " 'Yes, Lord; yet even the dogs under the table eat the children's crumbs' " (verse 28, R.S.V.).

"Then Jesus answered her, 'O woman, great is your faith! Be it done for you as you desire.' And her daughter was healed instantly" (Matt. 15:28, R.S.V.). And Mark records: " 'For this saying you may go your way; the demon has left your daughter.' And she went home, and found the child lying in bed, and the demon gone" (chap. 7:29, 30, R.S.V.).

Was this peaceful ending to a dramatic intrusion all that led Jesus to Syrophoenicia? Was that all that he dared to do among the Gentiles at that time? Did His primary mission "to the lost sheep of the house of Israel" limit His "foreign" labors? Did He leave it to His disciples and apostles to carry the gospel extensively to the Gentiles? We have questions, but no answers. Suffice it to say that although He primarily sought the sheep, His followers had His example for caring for the dogs under the table!

---

*L. H. Marshall, *St. Mark* (Grand Rapids, Eerdmans, 1968), p. 29.

CHAPTER 7

Early Shadow of a Cross

The Bible does not reveal two plans of salvation—one for the Hebrews of the Old Testament and a different one for the Jews-Christians of the New. The Prince of glory died on only one cross.

Those who lived before the cross had to look forward by faith. They showed their faith when they genuinely, in deep repentance for their sins, brought the required animal sacrifices to the altar of God (whether in the simple form of patriarchal times or in the later complex patterns of the tabernacle-temple days). Their actions demonstrated the principle that without the shedding of blood there is *no* forgiveness or blotting out of sins (Matt. 26:28; Heb. 9:22).

Those of us who live after the cross became a reality—with its bleeding Son of God victim—look backward in faith to the same sacrifice. It was and is equally efficacious for Hebrew and Christian forgiveness and salvation.

Although we will concentrate on the meaning of the cross in this chapter, we do not wish to overlook the necessity of Christ's life of perfect obedience to His father's will nor the necessity of His resurrection, ascension, intercession, and second coming to our salvation. But it seems that Christ Himself pointed to His cross as the pinnacle and as the essence of His incarnation. (Consider His conversation with Nicodemus in which He most thoroughly presented the plan of salvation with its symbol of the cross—"as Moses lifted up the serpent in the wilderness" [John 3:14, 15].)

At the cross Christ drank to the dregs the cup offered Him in Gethsemane. Without desiring in the least to belittle Calvary, the cup in Gethsemane contained the suffering of separation from God resulting from Christ's decision actually to bear on and in Himself the sins of the whole world.

Although we are talking of an early shadow of a cross that fell across the path Christ was treading in His ministry, we recognize that the shadow reaches back through the symbolic sacrificial system to the gates of Eden, to the inception of sin into our world, to the first promise of help for the race in its confrontation with the consequences of sin (Gen. 3:15). But still we have not traced it back far enough.

At some point in eternity past, there appeared the first hint of rebellion among the hosts of heaven. But does the dark shadow stop with the appearance of sin in the universe?

We now move to the limits of our own knowledge, logic, and reasoning, to where we may easily say more than we know. But with divine foreknowledge being as the Scriptures seemingly portray it—for example, in the whole area of predictive prophecy—we can scarcely put a point in eternity where the cross's shadow would not have fallen. How far back did the Godhead make the agreement to meet the possibility of sin? We cannot answer out of knowledge or Biblical evidence. But in some measure, the heart of God felt the pain of sin from eternity. Perhaps it is the most essential ingredient of the fullness of divine love.

But back to Mark and his flash pictures of the fast-moving events in the ministry of Jesus. We have reached a midpoint of emphasis. Up to now Jesus has been preaching the good news—proclamation. That does not stop here, but the approaching cross and all the suffering surrounding it join and overshadow it—the passion of the Christ.

According to Matthew and Mark Christ journeyed northward toward the villages of Caesarea Philippi. They do not record anything as taking place there, no event such as a healing. Perhaps Jesus simply sought a degree of privacy in which the great confession could be made. We might see that as an event of supreme significance—the acknowledgement by the apostles—through Peter as spokesman—as to the identity of their Master.

One may wonder why it took the twelve so long to know who their Master was, when the woman at Samaria, the Syrophoenician woman, and Mary Magdalene had remarkable insights into His mission when we consider their circumstances. But we need to remember how deeply ingrained were the Jews' expectations of the Messiah. They expected the prophecies of the kingdom of glory to be fulfilled at the *first* advent. And Christ simply did not fit their concept.

And so here is the conversation in part as it developed "on the way" (Mark 8:27, R.S.V.).

Christ: Who do men in general say that I am? What do they think of Me and My mission?

Disciples: Well, Master, many think you are John the Baptist come to life. You know, the people had a lot of faith in him—even some in high places.

Christ: Is that all?

Disciples: No, Master, no. Many others claim that you are Elijah, because of Malachi's prophecy and John's references to it.

Christ: And others?

Disciples: Well, yes, Master. Others say you are one of the great prophets returned or risen—like Moses, for example. He told of a prophet to come, like himself, to whom the people would listen. You know that, of course, Master.

Christ: But now, let Me come to what I most want to hear.

Disciples (eagerly and with wonder): Yes, Master.

Christ: Who do *you* say that I am?

A moment or two of hesitation followed. They realized the importance of His question to Him, so eagerly did His searching gaze scan each weatherworn face. The disciples fell silent, as if each hoped that another would answer. Why not Peter? He usually had an answer for everything. Some downcast eyes flitted upward long enough to suggest to him that he should speak. And then came the great confession: "Peter answered him, 'You are the Christ.' And he charged them to tell no one about him" (Mark 8:29, 30, R.S.V.).

Only Matthew records Christ's words of blessing and approval to Peter. His Gospel relates Peter—*petros,* a small rock or stone—to *petra,* a large rock or stone. Matthew also speaks of the keys of the kingdom and the authority entrusted by Christ to His apostles (Matt. 16:17-19, R.S.V.).

Tradition claims that Mark obtained his information about the life of Christ from Peter. Could Mark's more modest account reflect Peter's self-effacement? Is that reflected again by Luke, who is also silent about the keys to the kingdom?

We do not know where Christ was when He began to reveal the cross to His disciples. It could have been on His return to the region of Capernaum—his own city. But the important thing is that He began to confront their still-unprepared minds and imaginations with the fact that He, their Lord and Master, the One whom they had just acknowledged to be the Christ—the Anointed One, the Messiah—must soon suffer at the hands not of thieves and murderers, extortioners and terrorists, or even directly at the iron hand of Rome, but of the elders of the chosen people, their chief priests and the scribes.

And He was to be killed.

And after three days He would rise again.

Jesus took the time and effort to make this all very plain, clear, understandable, real! (Mark 8:31, 32).

Peter, whose mind the Holy Spirit had so recently enlightened so that he could declare Christ's true identity, mission, and purpose, now suddenly loses his sense of selfless dedication to Christ and the truth of the gospel. Temporarily he permits human fear of the most craven type to obsess his mind. For a moment he let Christ's persistent enemy control his thought and action.

The result is startling in the extreme. Peter takes hold of the Lord bodily. Doubtless he had a powerful build as a fisherman from using the crude boats, oars, sails, and nets of his trade. And you get the feeling that he actually took the Lord in his grasp, as though he could thus prevent Him from moving in the direction of the cross. As he seized Jesus physically, he exclaimed, "Be it far from thee, Lord: this shall not be unto thee" (Matt. 16:22).

Peter then received from his Lord, whom he loved with all his heart (but with imperfect understanding), one of the severest rebukes Jesus ever spoke to anyone. "Get thee behind me, Satan: thou are an offence unto me: for thou savourest not the things that be of God, but those that be of men" (verse 23).

No, Peter had not become demon possessed, nor was Satan speaking through Peter's vocal cords. It was that Satan was the source of the selfish and self-serving thought and motive that the disciple expressed. Satan hated the Christ and still more His cross. And yet he would not rest until the Saviour hung upon it.

Christ's patience with Peter at this time and over subsequent problems eventually broke the disciple's proud heart so that he could later advocate the joy of partaking of Christ's sufferings (1 Peter 4:12, 13). But just now he was not yet ready!

Mark, along with Matthew and Luke, for a moment moves the emphasis away from the projected cross of Christ. He bears down—in the words of the Lord Himself—upon the fact that every individual follower of Jesus has his or her own personal cross to carry, a knowledge He shared with "the multitude" also. In the process He completely inverted the Jewish scale of values. A concern for security, for gain, for profit consumed them. But Christ indicates that life itself—life eternal—has no basis of comparison in any earthly value. This is the ground for the teaching that if a man will seek first the kingdom of God and *His* righteousness, he will find all the temporal necessities added to him (Mark 8:34-9:1; cf. Matt. 6:33).

Then comes an interlude in the record of events. Mark relates the transfiguration of Christ and the healing of a demon-possessed boy (Mark 9:2-29). Right after that Mark, Matthew, and Luke each in his unique way portrays how Christ again insists to His little band of closest followers that He is indeed standing under the shadow of the cross. In Mark Jesus predicts His travesty of a trial, His death, and His resurrection the third day (verses 30-32). To Him it was as real as though it were beginning to happen. But the apostles had closed their minds against such possibilities. They did not understand and had no desire to probe, to enquire, to request a clarification. The Master was already bearing the cross alone—even when He only felt its early shadow!

CHAPTER 8

Judas the Expediter

Some modern theologians have argued that Jesus Christ really got Himself confused in the course of His mission on the earth. The world famous missionary to Africa, the late Dr. Albert Schweitzer, held the concept that Christ became confused or self-deceived in His closing months and sacrificed Himself to no avail.

In reality it is not a modern idea. We have seen in the previous chapter that Peter had no place for the cross in his scheme for the Messiah. And now we come to Judas. The most worldly-wise of the twelve, he was possibly the most talented, the natural leader. He was astute—or thought himself to be. And he harbored secret cynicism for the gullibility and simplemindedness (as he saw it) of his companions.

We are calling him Judas the expediter because he, too, had his own scenario for the Lord and it did not involve many of the things that Jesus did or permitted others to do. And he certainly had no place for a cross—either the Lord's or his own.

People naturally conjecture as to why Christ would invite a man like Judas Iscariot to be an apostle. It seems not to occur to us that Judas invited himself. That would certainly fit with everything else that we know from the Gospels that he did. He was a schemer, a slick operator, and he fancied himself as something of an entrepreneur. From *The Desire of Ages* (pages 293-295) we gather that he was of commanding appearance and intelligent. But Christ did not call him! The other disciples "sponsored" him to the Lord. And the Lord read him like a book—right to the back cover. Yet He took Judas in and gave him everything that He had given the rest.

Now we have to admit that the other eleven had their objectionable characteristics, too. The Saviour had to work with them patiently, steadily. But Judas was really a loner. A part of his heart he always reserved exclusively to himself. Even Christ was not welcome to enter it—and certainly neither were the dull wits that he perceived his comrades to be.

We all know that Judas carried the moneybag. There could not have been too much in it, but he managed to slip himself a little something on a fairly steady basis. Jesus knew it all and yet allowed him the responsibility in hope that what he saw and heard of Christ would yet reach him. He could have experienced repentance and reconcilation—as did Zacchaeus and Levi-Matthew. But Christ was careful not to challenge Judas too directly, and not publicly—pride always lurked too near the surface with him. He bristled easily. While he could hand out criticism, he could not take it graciously.

And now we come down to the end of Christ's brief sojourn in our sinful world. Some things had been accumulating in Judas' fertile brain. He resented some of the "failures" which Christ permitted to come to the cluster of early followers. Things happened that he would have planned differently, had Jesus sought and accepted his advice. Judas did not appreciate or even understand the many times Christ minimized those things that would have popular appeal. Christ's treasurer would have maximized them, especially if they involved people of wealth and influence.

Judas could conceive of himself as a man of discernment, a person with a sense of the political. The end would even justify the means for him. And he secretly despised the eleven for lacking what he saw as his own superior talent and sagacity.

His walk with Christ consisted of recurring crises, but not in the same way as with impetuous Peter, fiery John or James, or careful, painstaking Levi-Matthew. Rather Judas' crises came when in Judas' estimate Christ let certain opportunities slip through His fingers. He, Judas, would have made the test of the rich young ruler a little easier for the man to handle. Here was an opportunity to bring a man of wealth and influence into the apostolic circle. In his estimate Christ was just too slow on that one.

Then consider the times when the people got excited in support of Christ. They were even ready to take Him, by force if necessary, and knock out His overwhelming modesty by placing Him on the throne of the Jews. The masses would *make* Him king. When Christ ordered the disciples into a boat while He dispersed the crowds, it is not hard to imagine that Judas was the slowest at leaving, and the one who cast the most disparaging glances in the Lord's direction.

The approach of Jairus, the synagogue leader, and of the Roman centurion were occasions on which Judas would have tried to make both men conscious of their debt to Christ. Perhaps he might not have been too subtle in hinting that they owed the Lord a debt of gratitude—one of a tangible and substantial sort, of course—which he, Judas, would be glad to pass on.

The triumphal ride into Jerusalem more satisfied Judas's taste. The shouts of the multitudes, the untrammeled joy of the children, the strewn garments and symbolic palm branches were all in style for the event. It was just too bad that so many of the grateful "patrons" were also so desperately poor! In any case Jesus once again spoiled His glorious opportunity by suddenly weeping at the sight of the gold and marble of the Temple city. He was more concerned for the unbelieving people and their leaders than for any political advantage in the ground swell of popularity that the event offered.

But Judas had been troubled long before this over Christ's seeming lack of discernment—His lack of vision, opportunism, and leadership. His presentation of Himself as the Bread of Life had turned many of His followers away from Him. Judas deeply regretted Jesus' undiplomatic move.

The eventual betrayer had tried repeatedly to get Christ to recognize and follow the wise lines he had laid out to the throne. We can easily see him behind the efforts to take Christ by force and make him king! Christ's power to heal, to raise the dead, to feed thousands from one small lunch, were all practical factors that would fit into Judas' schemes for a temporal kingdom.

If we wonder how Judas could eventually betray his Lord for thirty pieces of silver, we must come to see that act as a logical piece in his overall plan. He must force Christ to declare His identity, to put His overworked humility aside. Jesus must finally do what His disciple had decided He must really be wanting to do.

Let us not forget the prominent role Judas played in complaining about the profligate waste (as he claimed to see it) of Mary Magdalene's costly gift to Christ at Simon's house—Simon the leper, Simon the Pharisee. It is conceivable that at the moment he was complaining of Mary's extravagance he had already made an initial agreement with Christ's bitterest enemies to betray Him (compare Mark 14:1, 2, 10, 11 with verses 3-9).

At our safe distance from the time of Christ it may seem incredible that Judas could have any worthy motive in betraying the Lord. And perhaps it is questionable to use the word "worthy" in this setting. But such is the subtle corrosion of reasoning power and moral sensitivity when self-indulgence and self-seeking dominate the life that "to do evil that good may come" seems not only feasible but desirable, and even right.

John specifies what the other Gospel writers generalize about Mary's gift. He makes Matthew's "his disciples" (chap. 26:8) and Mark's "some" (chap. 14:4) into "Judas Iscariot, one of his disciples" (chap. 12:4, R.S.V.), which leads to the thought that on this occasion Judas acted as spokesman for one or more of the disciples. And why not? As treasurer he would encourage complaint over expenditures on anything short of what was essential.

But even treasurers are not always logical, and how is it with Judas here? Mary has some money—perhaps the equal of a year's wages—and she has saved it and kept it for something special. Now, under the prompting of a Spirit-filled heart of love for her Redeemer, she has lavished the whole sum on a costly quantity of oil or ointment of pure nard. She has come in where she might have reason to feel unwelcome, embarrassed, even ashamed, and despite that, she has poured out her love with her gift upon the Saviour's feet as He sat at the table in Simon's house.

Now Judas wants to know why she did not sell the ointment and give the proceeds to the poor—through, of course, the moneybag that he carried. Why buy the ointment only to sell it again! He was really complaining to Christ indirectly that He should not have permitted her to make this intruding gift. Was Judas expecting Christ to have prevented Mary from making her rather secret purchase? What other logic is there in the complaint of Judas and his fellow grumblers?

It would be tempting to indulge in sarcastic ridicule of such paltry thinking, but the situation is too redolent with heaven-inspired love. The Saviour is about to say something that Judas will resent. And the disciple will allow his resentment to fester until he will decide to show Christ a thing or two!

Remember the concept of the Messiah bred into the Jewish mind and tradition from infancy and for centuries? All the allusions to world domination, to the kingdom of glory being given to the saints of the Most High, to ruling the nations with a rod of iron—all of that and more is to come with the Messiah. Judas, in common with his fellow disciples, has that type of expectation of the Anointed One. Yet during the recent months Christ has made repeated efforts to let His disciples know that He is to go to Jerusalem shortly, to be put on trial there, to suffer physical and mental torture, and finally to die on a cross and be raised from the dead the third day. Unfortunately none of it sinks in. (Go back, if need be, to Mark 8:31-33. The account is there.)

So Judas does not believe that Jesus will really let Himself be killed as predicted. But if Christ wants to insist on it, Judas will capitalize on the hatred of the Jewish leadership for Him. He, Judas, will make a deal with the Jewish leadership to betray Christ to a motley crowd of police, soldiers, and riffraff at a time when the populace will not be present to intervene in behalf of their Benefactor.

So, as he lays his subplot to the Jewish plot, Judas sees thirty pieces of silver as a net gain. He will do his part, but, as so many times before, Christ will walk out of the hands of His enemies. If He does not, He will have to take the consequences. With all the powers Christ has shown, Judas knows He can escape.

More than that, when it comes right down to facing His own suffering and death, Judas believes that Christ will finally reveal Himself for what Judas believes that He is—the King of the Jews. And he, Judas the expediter, will modestly accept the world's praise and Christ's praise for having the insight and willingness to force Him into a situation in which He would *have* to reveal Himself and His power rather than to go to the cross.

Only such a scenario could account for Judas' dramatic actions. But they did not work as he had anticipated. First, Jesus made no attempt to deliver Himself from the mob. Though He did question why Judas would choose to betray the Son of man with a kiss (Luke 22:48). When Peter tried a clumsy defense, Christ intervened to stop him and to repair the damage done. But when Judas saw that Christ asked only for protection for His disciples and permitted the mob to bind Him and lead Him away, the disciple's world of cleverness fell in upon him.

He could think only of the upper room, of Christ's willingness to wash His betrayer's feet and to permit him a place at His table. A flood of other memories swept in, and they all confirmed the prediction of Christ: "One of you shall betray me." And it was he, Judas himself, and no other. All the eleven—even Peter—ran from the garden, forsaking their Lord. Judas could not know that Peter had denied Him. He was too busy with his own torturing conscience.

Angry with himself and sensing desperate depths of guilt and stupidity, Judas turned his anger and accusations against the men in holy office who had gladly conspired with an apostle for his Master's betrayal. His dramatic flinging of the thirty pieces of silver down at the throne of the high priest in the Temple area and his choking acknowledgement that he had betrayed innocent blood brought him no deliverance from his own accusing conscience.

And Judas, the utterly selfish "expediter," found a rope and hanged himself. Apparently the rope broke at some point, and the Jerusalem sanitary corps—the dogs—moved in to sanitize the area (compare Matt. 27:5 with Acts 1:16-19 and *The Desire of Ages,* p. 722).

CHAPTER 9

Why a Triumph?

One of the mysteries of Christ's earlier ministry was His repeated instruction to those benefited by His miracles that they should keep to themselves what He had done for them. It must have puzzled the disciples, because Jesus came into Galilee at the outset of His ministry declaring the time fulfilled at which the kingdom of God would be "at hand." John the Baptist's mission had been to prepare the Lord's way. Then why the persistent reticence?

At times during Christ's ministry a cynic could have claimed that a kind of tokenism marked it. Visiting the pool of Bethesda, He chose only one among presumably scores of sufferers to heal (an event recorded only in the Gospel of John [5:1-18]). As we have already seen, Scripture records Jesus helping only one person during His journey into Tyre and Sidon territory. He asked the lepers and blind persons He healed not to blaze His name abroad as their benefactor. Sometimes it was to protect the person so he could meet the requirement of a priestly affidavit of healing and return to society and to the Temple worship. But in general, why the reluctance and seeming secrecy? (On a number of occasions those involved did not follow Christ's instructions. They did indeed blaze His name far and wide, and the multitudes came flocking. See, for example, Mark 1:45; 7:36.)

Actually, these were occasions when Christ deliberately acted to cool the ardor of the multitudes and of His own disciples. We have earlier noted the crisis in Galilee when the people and the disciples determined to make Him a king by force (John 6:15-17; cf. Mark 6:45-52). Jesus sent His disciples away by boat, and He dismissed the eager crowds.

But somewhere in Christ's ministry comes a change. It is not that the old reasons for caution and restraint have disappeared, or that Jewish prejudice has changed. Rather, in spite of it, the multitudes must receive every opportunity to see evidence of Christ's Messiahship. He must do everything possible to free the minds of God's people from the domination of Jewish tradition. They must be able to see the character of God as it really is—as revealed by the One who was the express or exact image of the Father.

Jesus must also draw the attention of the people to the last footsteps in the path taken to Calvary. There must be a multitude of eyewitnesses safe from the deceptions put forward by the nation's leaders. And this is the context in which the question in the title of this chapter must find its answer—"Why a triumph?"

We use the term here in a special sense. Usually a triumph followed a great military or naval victory in which the victorious general, prince, king, or emperor brought his captives home. He spared certain ones of the enemy so that he could parade them before the madly cheering masses lining the route of his return to the capital city.

Sometimes the victor would allow his greatest enemies to live because of the respect between great warriors or because an earlier conqueror had done a similar favor to the new hero. Other times, however, the winner had the enemy leaders paraded in shame and led to torture and death.

The people usually went delirious in celebrating the

triumph, sometimes acting as though forsaken of all reason. At times it meant that the conquering armies brought home the wealth of an enemy nation to share to some degree with all loyal citizens. Always it indicated the superiority of the fighting legions and the brilliance of their commanders over their enemies. Sometimes it offered a rare occasion for rejoicing in an otherwise dull, difficult, and painful fight for existence. But why a triumph headed by the Man of Galilee? The answer comes in a number of parts.

A few paragraphs earlier we noted the change that came in Christ's public ministry. His former reticence bordering on secrecy changed to an open presentation of all that He said and did. Jesus took longer routes to nearby destinations that He might draw the attention of all possible to the series of events that would culminate in a crown of thorns and a wooden cross. Such an end could well be served by a triumph! The Lord set the processes in motion with a few simple commands—and it was as though Providence ordained all that followed.

Christ did not choose from one of the lines of horses made famous in the stables of Solomon. That would not have been uniquely Jewish. Neither would it have fulfilled the details of Zechariah's prophecy: "Rejoice greatly, O daughter of Zion; shout, O daughter of Jerusalem: . . . he is just, and having salvation; lowly, and riding upon an ass, and upon a colt the foal of an ass" (Zech. 9:9).

The triumphal procession took place on a Sunday, and some of us remember from childhood the crosses made of straw or raffia—a cultivated palm from Madagascar, the leaf stalks of which furnish fiber for making hats, mats, baskets—and given to the children on Palm Sunday of each year in commemoration of His ride. Incidentally, hosts of people entered Jerusalem at this time of the year. The Passover was about to be celebrated, and Jews both of the Diaspora (scattered among the nations) and those from lesser distances gathered for the sacred, solemn, and festal services.

In His simple instructions to two of His disciples Jesus showed again His dependence upon those who believed His message and mission in some way. They were to enter a village near Bethphage, on the Mount of Olives, and find an ass tied with her colt. Untying the creatures, they would bring them to Him. If anyone questioned them, they should tell him only that the Lord had need of the animals. Matthew says the result would be that the owner would send the animals immediately, and Mark has the disciples assuring the owners that the colt (which the Lord chose for the ride) would be sent back immediately (Matt. 21:1-3 and Mark 11:1-6).

In either case, Luke and John confirm that it was the foal, or colt, on which the Lord chose to ride. One wonders how the beast submitted to a carpenter riding bareback on it for the first time ever. Was it another act of faith, or are ass colts born "broken"? We might be inclined today to smile behind our hands at such a primitive method to display the Lord before His people and the world. But if the method of riding was traditional of Jewish kings, we can understand that as He took His seat a shout of triumph would split the air and that a steady crescendo of sound and people would join the happy throng.

The poor had no great gifts to offer the King. But they had strong voices for shouting. They usually had some outer garment to lay in the dusty trail for the Lord to ride over, and low-spreading tree branches to wave. And the triumph was on!

But now the major question. Who were the captives riding or staggering along in *His* train? There could be some extraordinary persons on display that day—and all voluntarily, in great joy, in unfettered love. How about the person leading Christ's colt, who had been dead in his grave four days?* How about cured lepers laying a carpet before His beast? How about the loudest shouts coming from those once deaf and dumb? How about the lame, who competed with each other in leaping for joy and turning cartwheels in His honor? How about Satan's most helpless victims now proclaiming with sanctified joy the name of their Deliverer? See the radiant faces and tear-brimmed eyes of the widows and orphans who now had a family—the other sons and daughters of God.

Never was there a triumph like it. Only when the King of kings rides His chariot of clouds and angels at the last trump can another compare to it. Palm Sunday is but a dim foretaste of the glory of the Lord.

Suddenly the procession slowed, and angry voices began to protest. Religious leaders suddenly appeared in an attempt to break up the demonstration before the whole world went delirious in praise of Him. They were concerned that the procession had assembled without an official permit from the Sanhedrin or from the Roman governor. It suited their hypocritical purposes now. But the Lord's answer showed the folly of their hypocritical whining. Look, He said, if I tell these people to hush, these paving stones lying around will start to shout what the people are saying. Will you have the stones arrested?

Nothing in this world is more powerful than a Bible prophecy whose time has come. It was time for this demonstration—prophecy called for it, men could not prevent it. So, He whose reputation had been spreading through the Jewish dispersion during the short years of His ministry was now the name on every tongue, the topic of every conversation, the subject of every inquiry.

The petrified authorities shrank back into the shadows as the triumph rolled on. Who could stop it? Who is this? was the cry from the thousands coming out from the city to meet Him, and the crowds accompanying Him knew! " 'Blessed is the kingdom of our father David that is coming! Hosanna in the highest!'" (Mark 11:10, R.S.V.).

And as suddenly, the triumph came to a complete halt as its Subject-object halted, an incident that only Luke records. Was Jesus, like the people, overwhelmed by the beauty of the domed and pinnacled Temple as its glistening marble and gold began to reflect the glory of the westering sun? Did it move Him to tears?

But soon from the depths of His swaying form they heard the awesome words of a deep lament. Words cannot paint the colors or sounds of the scene. Have you ever seen and heard a man who weeps for his dead wife or child? There is no sound like it.

Now the Lord of glory sways as before a tempest. His eyes burn with tears, and from quivering lips comes the broken cry, "Would that even today you knew the things that make for peace!" [He told of the city's destruction] "because you did not know the time of your visitation!" (Luke 19:41-44, R.S.V.).

Not because of the Romans did Jerusalem die forty years after His triumph. Her own persistent myopia made it impossible for her to see her Lord when He was in her very midst. Jerusalem's day of opportunity departed with Him.

That's why there was a triumph. All Israel and the strangers near and far must ultimately know that Israel destroyed herself.

---

* *The Desire of Ages,* p. 572.

CHAPTER 10

Under Secret Orders

Military men everywhere, especially in times of war, often operate under secret orders. Only the highest echelons of their commanders and their government are supposed to know the secret plans and objectives.

The church of God is a militant body that operates universally under the direction of the Captain of the Lord's host. He has under His command a vast army of angel couriers continually being dispatched on missions that are secret from the rulers of our world. The Holy Spirit, the personal representative of the Lord of hosts, is universally present with the human units fighting the battles of the King of kings and Lord of lords. And all are operating on timed plans that will culminate in the restoration of universal and eternal peace in our sin-invaded world and universe.

When the Lord was here in person, he established the organization and leadership of His church militant under twelve apostles. How He could have had the courage to leave His cause in such faltering hands as theirs almost defies human understanding. But their hearts were His, and He promised the Holy Spirit *(paraklētos)* to provide all the power they would ever need. It would be as though Christ Himself dwelt within each Christian soldier.

Their Captain provided His twelve chosen men hands-on training and instruction in the field and in the classroom. They studied theory, and He gave them opportunities for practice. He sent them out alone on military maneuvers, promising them power to meet the enemy in open combat. Their power was in His name (Mark 6:6-13).

The twelve had a deeply ingrained problem, however, in getting a clear understanding of the real nature of the kingdom Christ had come to restore. The archenemy of Christ, who had initiated the first rebellion against His authority in heaven, had been working long and devotedly by means of fifth columns and brainwashing techniques to confuse that people whom Christ had specially chosen on the earth.

Thus on many occasions the disciples simply did not understand their Lord or His orders. His disinterest in the political support that the Jewish leadership could have offered Him puzzled them. If only He had shaped His cause and His own conduct more in harmony with their expectations (verses 45-52).

So toward the end of His ministry Christ, in His role as Prophet, began to reveal to the Jewish leaders something of their future. On one such occasion He referred to the Temple as their's rather than God's and indicated that when He left its precincts, it would be *their* house and would soon be desolated (Matt. 23:38).

As the disciples followed their Lord from the massive edifice that was the Temple of Yahweh they called His attention to the enormous mass of the stones forming the walls and the meticulous precision by which they were laid. And more than a little national pride and some measure of disbelief lurked in their tones as they reacted to Christ's indication of the fate of the glorious city of Jerusalem. Matthew's account, in chapter 24:1, 2, sounds almost as though the disciples took Him around it to show Him the enormous strength of the Temple's foundations and walls as an argument that His predictions could not possibly come about. Who, or what force, could possibly dislodge those massive stones that had withstood earlier sieges?

The Lord dropped the matter as long as the crowds were around, but later, as He sat on the crest of the Mount of Olives, four of His closest disciples approached Him with a composite question. In the process of answering it, Jesus gave to His church militant her *secret orders* that would direct her from that moment to His second coming to this earth.

When one considers the seeming ineptitude and unsuitability of the skills and personalities of most of the twelve for the task at hand, one wonders how Christ could have thought to entrust the future and final fruition of His mission to such a group of incompetents. Of course, the Father and the Holy Spirit guided Him in all such matters. But really there must be two keys to the ultimate triumph of the church: (1) her faithfulness to the secret orders of Bible prophecy, and (2) her openness to and dependence upon the indwelling presence and transforming power of the Holy Spirit.

In chapter 1 we referred to the work of L. E. Froom on the history of prophetic interpretation. We would point out, as Froom did, that the rise and fall of the expectation of Christ's second coming has varied with the clarity of the church's understanding of five key factors involving the prophetic portions of the Bible—and especially the apocalyptic books, Daniel and the Revelation. They are: (1) the outline prophecies, (2) the resurrection, (3) the millennium, (4) the antichrist, and (5) the visible kingdom of God.

Now the secret orders that Christ entrusted to four of His closest followers (and that, with minor variations, Matthew 24, Mark 13, and Luke 21 record) parallel the projection of history in advance as given by Daniel and John the Revelator. Our study will concentrate on the presentation given by Mark.

It is doubtful that the four disciples had more than a vague impression and understanding of what Christ had said of the future. Neither is it likely that they had clear-cut issues in mind when they asked their questions. More likely their curiosity had been aroused regarding the future, and they may have been more concerned about the overthrowing of the sacred Temple than anything else. Nevertheless, they voiced questions upon which Christ could base His outline of secret orders for His church.

(The fact that we observe some differences in Matthew, Mark, and Luke as to exactly who asked Jesus the questions—and also as to their exact wording—need not trouble us unduly. The discourse that follows in each case is sufficiently close to the other two to point to a common event and setting, but with many variations and emphases.)

The question cluster presented to Christ as recorded by the three gospel accounts includes several elements:

1. When will the Temple be overthrown?
2. What signs will show this event near?
3. What will be the signs of Your coming?
4. What will be the signs of the approaching end of the age?

In answering them Jesus did not completely separate and delineate the several elements. It was something that the order in which the events took place would eventually clarify, as would the fulfillment of the promise that the Spirit of truth would guide the believers into all truth (John 16:12-15).

First came a warning of the kind of treatment that the apostolic church would experience immediately upon the launching of her mission. Also He foretold the climate in which the church would begin its mission. Many false Christs and false prophets would seek to confuse this infant church just bereft of her Lord. She would find herself caught in political turmoil and conflict between nations and would suffer persecution. Extraordinary physical phenomena would occur on earth and in the heavens.

But as Mark records, Christ's followers were not to be "anxious beforehand" concerning what they would say. The Holy Spirit would give them words to speak. The church would witness bitter incidents of betrayal of believer by believer—even within families. But he who endured would be saved (Mark 13:11-13, R.S.V.). And all have a gospel commission to fulfill, one sweeping on to the Second Coming.

Then in full chorus Matthew, Mark, and Luke go back to give Christ's warning on how Jerusalem would be destroyed. They also give His secret orders, which, if followed faithfully, would preserve all the believers (Matt. 24:15-20; Mark 13:14-18; Luke 21:20-22). If the besieging armies withdrew temporarily before attacking, that would give the Christian believers precious moments to leave the Holy City before its dreadful destruction.

The first three Gospels each mention days of tribulation and distress. Days that would have to be shortened to prevent the complete destruction of the saints (Mark 13:20). Immediately following, and even during, the closing ones of those days there would be signs—in the earth and in the heavens—to show the imminence of the coming of the Lord.

We take the above secret orders and search the lives and events of history to which they could most fully apply. The 1260 days of Revelation and of Daniel also come to mind. And we observe in history a power that endures that long and does to the true believers all that Jesus foretold. Then its power to persecute the saints is reduced, foreshortened by the rising intelligence and independence of thought of the birth of learning following the Dark Ages. Next, the glory of the Reformation blocks the Papacy-Antichrist, greatly diminishing its reign before the 1798 climax of the 1260 days.

Though the Lord does not give any comparative numbers, He leaves us with the strong impression that 1798 begins the time of the end, and that events will move comparatively quickly toward "the Son of man coming in clouds with great power and glory" (verse 26, R.S.V.).

Was He still blending the two events—Jerusalem's end and that of the world—in His words about a generation that would not pass away "before all these things take place" (verse 30, R.S.V.). Some of the generation to which He spoke doubtless saw Jerusalem's destruction.

But the clearest understanding of the secret orders for the church will not reveal the day and hour of the Lord's return. Hence the warning to " 'watch therefore—for you do not know when the master of the house will come, in the evening, or at midnight, or at cockcrow, or in the morning—lest he come suddenly and find you asleep. And what I say to you I say to all: Watch' " (verses 35-37, R.S.V.).

This is the most vital secret order of all!

CHAPTER 11

Heaven Hushed to Listen

The crisis of the ages—of eternity—is settled amid the spreading olive trees in the garden known as Gethsemane on the slope of the Mount of Olives, overlooking the Temple, and possibly Calvary. The scenario amid the gnarled branches forever resolves the controversy between truth and error, life and death, sin and righteousness. Any lingering question in the mind of the universe regarding the benevolence and justice of God's government and law vanishes there. The fact that our sins, taken upon Him by choice and in love, were crushing out the life of our Saviour—without a cross—is clear. Calvary implements what Gethsemane decides. And all the universe hushed to listen.

Throughout His short life on earth, and particularly through the three years of His ministry, the Saviour was continually in prayer. Rising early in the morning or slipping away in the evening, He made the hills His refuge and His temple. There He communed with His God, gaining renewal of spiritual strength and power to meet whatever each day would present before Him. Often He agonized in prayer to His Father in behalf of certain needy individuals, some very close to Him who were particular targets of Satan. But now all is different, for He prays for Himself.

He begs for the sympathetic understanding of His closest friends and supporters. Jesus has taken all twelve—except Judas—to the Garden. But wanting a smaller group with Him, He takes the three present at the transfiguration. They had seen and heard Moses and Elijah communing with Him, had witnessed their Lord glorified with some measure of that which was His by divine right. Now Jesus will take the three to the place of decision. Repeatedly He has chosen them to participate in a special relationship with Himself. Not intended to make them conceited or self-righteous, it had been to prepare them for this His dreadful hour and for what would follow the cross.

Peter, James, and John. Remarkable! The mother of the latter two had tried to corner the two highest places in the kingdom for her sons. They were good boys and she was a good mother. The Zebedees were doubtless more generous than most in meeting the needs of the Christ and His little band. At the time, Jesus had asked them if they could drink His cup and receive His baptism. They believed they could, and He said they would. But the highest places were not His to give. Yet, here they are, plus Peter. The Saviour needs them desperately now. Needs their prayers, their love, their support, their understanding. Craving human friendship, He just needs to know that somebody cares!

Why is He who has always been so strong, so weak and uncertain now—almost disoriented and under dreadful stress? Groaning, moaning, weaving, staggering—as under a terrible, crushing burden. It is the terrible weight of the sins of the whole human race, past, present, and future. They bear down on Him as though to press Him into the very rocks of the ground.

From eternity He has looked forward to this hour. But now it is here. A man may wait on death row for years. His fears blow hot and cold as people set dates, then stay his execution. But one day it is for real. They have shaved his head. He has had a breakfast of his own choosing. A clergyman visits him. And now the officers conduct him on the longest walk of his life. It may be only fifty paces or twelve. But when he has taken them, he will die.

Sometimes criminals scream and struggle with their guards. But Jesus controls His fate. He would not have to die. Christ could decline to drink the cup. Wishing His three closest followers would join Him in prayer, He asks them to. But He cannot abide that they should see His grief and He staggers deeper into the Garden.

Jesus cries out to His Father, almost in desperation, yet in faith. He wants to be delivered from the awful sense of separation and rejection. Can't someone share His burden? Stumbling back to His three disciples, He finds them sprawled grotesquely in deep sleep, the hoods of their garments pulled up over their heads to keep out the night's cold.

Nobody, nobody, nobody! There is nobody to drink the cup with Him or even to encourage Him in swallowing it. Nobody except Him seems to care about the cup. It clings to His hands as though magnetized. He cannot free Himself from it. "Oh my Father, can't you take this cup away from Me? Do I *have* to drink it? Is there no other way to save these sinners?" But the Father, and all heaven, is hushed.

And the adversary whispers that He should not waste Himself on such heedless sinners. Who will accept the benefits of His atonement anyway? A handful at best. Even all the disciples are sleeping. No one really cares. Not even His Father!

Yet He can't believe that—He won't believe it. He thinks back over all the steps that He has taken in thirty-three years, and He knows the Father has never forsaken Him. Jesus remembers the renewal of power for Himself and needy humanity that He has received day and night from His Father. The audible voice at the baptism, the descending dove, the voice at the Temple when the Greeks came, all flood back to His mind. Why can He not keep these things sharply in focus? Why is it such a struggle?

Almost numb and senseless, He slumps to the ground. Reaching out His arms and hands upon the cold earth, He grasps at it with His fingers as though to anchor Himself—to hold Himself back from the pit into which sin would seem to plunge Him.

How long has He prayed? How long has He struggled? It seems an eternity. But He revives to a sense of why He is here. He remembers the cup. That is the issue. Will He drink it? Will He take it? Will He accept to Himself the sins of a whole world—He who knew no sin?

That was why He came. That is why he is in Gethsemane. Calvary is across the slope somewhere. "Father, if Your will can be done only when I drink this cup of humanity's guilt and loss—I will drink. I will take it. Give it to Me." And an angel assumes the place the apostles might have had. His presence assures that Heaven cares. All heaven has hushed to listen for His decision. In that waiting silence He has made His choice known, and the angel comes to keep Him from dying there in the garden—to strengthen Him to go forward to Calvary. "As Moses lifted up the serpent . . ." It seemed a long time since He had explained it to Nicodemus. But the decision has been made. The cup has been taken. He will bear the sins of many, for the Lord has laid on Him the iniquity of us all.

Why is heaven so concerned for the fate of one man in a garden on the edge of Jerusalem? Why is every harp hushed, every song silenced? Why has all heaven waited with baited breath for the agonizing struggle in Gethsemane? Three times the cup has been presented. Twice the fainting victim has shown His yearning to escape the awful contents of that mysterious vessel. Is He going to decline? It is evident He wants to. He longs for His Father to offer some other way to save the human race from annihilation.

But again, why was heaven so concerned for the outcome of the struggle in Gethsemane's garden? Was it just for the comparative few out of the billions of humanity who would respond to the sacrifice of eternal love and be restored to an earth made over new for their eternal habitation?

No, it was for far more than this. How much more we may not fully understand until instructed by God Himself. But if Christ had failed in the final and infinite demonstration of the utter selflessness of God's nature, character, and government, could heaven itself ever have been secure again?

Would the questions that had lingered even in the minds of the loyal angels and the inhabitants of unfallen worlds have intensified if Christ had failed. Would it have seemed to confirm and substantiate Satan's claim to have taken over the "dominion" entrusted to Adam? Would it have been made permanent? Would this one dark spot in the universe of God have remained forever so?

If Christ ran the risk of failure and eternal loss in coming to our world, Gethsemane was certainly the final hour of decision. The Saviour had won all earlier contests, but the Garden was the final challenge. If the adversary did not succeed here, it would tear his mask away and reveal him for all time as just what Jesus said he was—a liar, a murderer.

But there may be a deeper dimension yet in the risks Heaven took in sending Christ. He came to demonstrate, in humanity, that the law of God—the law that is fulfilled by love—was sound, fair, and possible to obey throughout all of God's creation. Christ's life must be a perfect and blameless demonstration. Should He have failed in one particular, would it have put the government of heaven in jeopardy? Would it have weakened the authority of God forever? Inspiration is not too specific on such issues, but does portray a day to come in which every knee will bow before Christ in fear—godly or otherwise, saving or destructive.

Arising from the earth, the Saviour goes out to His sleeping followers. There He awakens them to meet the mob that even now is crashing through the garden with swords and staves and torches. In the lead is Judas Iscariot, one of His own, now cooperating with the priests and Temple police.

The cantata declares:

"Then all, all His disciples
forsook Him
and fled."

But the end is not yet.

CHAPTER 12

Immeasurable Measure

We have no way to measure the love of God that Jesus showed to the universe on a cruel Roman cross. Nor can we calculate the hate and cruelty flung at Christ's innocence.

This making the decision to drink the cup of our woe in Gethsemane did not reduce the fierce, demented anger of men and demons that would have torn Him limb from limb before He could be nailed to the cross.

The complete picture of the immeasurable sufferings of Christ for our sins has to include every moment of His walk on earth. The incomparable innocence and purity of His perfect life roused the ire of all who would not yearn to be like Him and to be saved by His grace. Above all, it made Him the constant target of the powers of darkness under the leadership of one who had been next to Christ in the heavenly ranks.

That Christ actually would dare to come alone to the claimed domain of the great deceiver, with the deliberate intent to rob him of his captives and to let the oppressed go free Satan could not let go unchallenged. Thus he flung the most seductive psychological, physical, and spiritual tests imaginable at Him in quick succession. Hours of courtroom hazing, military brutality, and support group disloyalty were all part of the immeasurable measure of the Lord's sufferings. But none of these in itself caused His death.

There is not an easy or natural division between the agony of Gethsemane and that of Calvary. In essence they were one and the same except that Gethsemane involved the additional agony of making a decision. The stark question was whether He who came to be man's redeemer would actually *choose* to complete the task or not. With the decision made, Calvary was the inevitable end, bringing with it the trauma of the trials, mockings, and scourgings not to mention the denials and forsakings by those on whose loyalty He had counted.

The events from the upper room/Passover/Lord's Supper experiences onward flow and merge together into an increasing crescendo. At the upper room meal Jesus revealed to Judas that He was aware of every step that he had taken and of his plot to betray his Lord to His bitterest enemies. The fact that Judas may never have believed that Jesus would not deliver Himself from His enemies does not reduce the horror of such an act of betrayal. As Jesus said (Mark 14:21), The Son of man would die for the sins of the whole world, but that did not reduce the guilt and woe of the man who would be willing to betray the Lord of glory!

The Passover Supper with His closest followers was His last food until after the resurrection. He would have no sleep that night or until He died nearly twenty hours later.

Perhaps the betrayal by Judas was more endurable to the Lord than what Peter did to Him within a few hours of the Last Supper. After all, Judas had never made a full commitment to Christ. Peter, on the other hand, had been one of the first to follow the Lord (chap. 1:16-18), and he had become a natural leader and the general spokesman among the apostles. He forcefully proclaimed his loyalty to Christ and his fearlessness in the face of whatever might come to his Lord. But again, he was expressing the conviction of the group. They all testified of their loyalty and fearlessness in the face of death (chap. 14:31)!

Then came Judas, the betrayer, and a motley multitude instigated by the high priest of Israel and the scribes and elders (verse 43). When one considers the sacredness originally associated with the high priest's person, garments, character, and ministry, it seems incredible that one in the line of succession could have fallen so low as to see Christ as his rival and to plot to destroy Him by any means possible.

In quick succession, then, came the fleeing of the eleven, Christ's attempts to protect them, the strange little incident about a young man who might have been John Mark himself (verses 50-52), Peter's denial at the palace of the high priest, and the first of a series of travesties on the power and authority of Jewish law and justice.

The Jewish leadership was in a real and multiple dilemma. If they were to succeed in having this Man put to death by the Roman authorities and guards, they must prove Him to have broken a Roman law that carried the death penalty. It must, of course, do the same according to Jewish law, but the leadership felt that they could readily find a suitable excuse. Had they not, on several occasions, accused Christ of blasphemy for making Himself an equal with God? That itself would bring Him the Jewish verdict of death (verses 61-64).

We shall not linger here over the succession of trials and punishments for crimes not proved, or the tragic weaknesses of the Roman governor, Peter the apostle, or Herod, tetrarch of Galilee (Luke 23:6-12). Each of them was guilty of adding to Jesus' immeasurable sufferings. What men were there worthy of the death He would soon suffer?

But He pressed on to the cross. The faith strengthened through thirty-three years of perfect submission to His Father's will must not fail Him now. His own avowed disciples were in terrible disarray—except for the women, including His mother and Mary Magdalene. They stood "looking on afar off" (Mark 15:40). Eventually John must have drawn nearer and supported the fainting form of Jesus' mother. She doubtless still could not understand why her Son had come to this. But she had not forsaken Him. The predicted sword was truly piercing her own soul now, more cruelly than ever before (Luke 2:33-35). And Jesus? Could He have any place in His mind for His mother's suffering when the sins of the whole world were now crushing Him? For every man who remembers his own mother's sufferings and prayers in his behalf, His words to her are enough to break the heart with bursts of love: "Woman, behold thy son!" To His disciple John he said, "Behold thy mother!" And according to John's own account, "that disciple took her unto his own home" (John 19:26, 27). The meaning is not only that he took her to his dwelling place but he took her as though she were *his* mother, welcomed her into his heart.

The end then came swiftly. It took everyone by surprise. A frightening darkness had enclosed the cross and the country around for three hours. The centurion had never heard of anyone dying in only six hours. It wasn't the cross, the nails, the iron-tipped lashings, or the hunger and thirst that killed Him. The pious rantings and railings of priests, scribes, and rabbis did not slay Him. Nor did the cry of the people to have the crook Barabbas released nor the frenzied, fanatic chant "Crucify him, crucify him." None of those things slew Him, though they would have eventually.

His enemies could not believe Him *dead.* They did not want Him to come down from the cross. Had He, they would have scattered like a flock of chickens. But soon they would wish Him all the way back to heaven! Indeed, it would be as though He had come down from the cross.

He would soon return to life, and they remembered His declaration that He would.

No, Jesus died of His own choice. He laid down His life voluntarily. No one took it from Him. (Not even the soldier who thrust the point of a spear into His side.) Christ died of a broken heart. His Father had to forsake His Son while the Son bore our sins upon the tree. The first separation in all eternity between Father and Son was the immeasurable measure of His love. The price of our sins. And Jesus paid it in full!

CHAPTER 13

He's Gone—But He's Still Here!

A contemporary religious song repeatedly asks where Jesus is. And as repeatedly the answer comes back that He is no longer at Bethlehem, the Jordan River, Gethsemane, or Calvary, but is gone. And that is the glorious truth that will consume our thought in the first half of our final chapter. "He's gone."

Christianity has many unique aspects as it stands among all the world religions. But none more so than Christ's empty tomb.

The fifteenth chapter of Mark's Gospel closes with a combination of sad and joyous episodes blending together in the story line. Jesus has with triumphant trumpet tones declared to the hushed universe that His work for man's salvation is finished. The price has been paid in full! "IT IS FINISHED" (John 19:30).

After committing His life into the Father's hands (Luke 23:46) He died. None can harm Him or defeat His purpose now. His death made Him a conqueror.

As was customary in those days, the followers of a martyr—like those of John the Baptist—consider it part of their privilege to bury whatever remains of their leader. But the disciples of Jesus are poor, generally uninfluential, and utterly terrified. They are sure that the fate of their Lord awaits each of them. In this desperate hour two men of wealth, influence, and immunity to both Jewish and Roman pressure came forward. Between them,

Joseph of Arimathaea and Nicodemus (both respected members of the Sanhedrin) provide a cave tomb with a massive stone door, a hundred pounds of myrrh and aloes (reminiscent of Mary's earlier gift of nard to the living Christ), and a clean linen shroud in which to wrap the body of our Lord (see Mark 15:42-47 and compare it with John 19:38-42).

At least two of the women from Galilee watched the procedures—the wrapping and placing of the body within the tomb, the rolling of the great circular stone in its trough (hewn out of rock) to close the tomb (Mark 15:47). Then all went their various ways to rest according to the Sabbath commandment.

The next day after Jesus' friends had departed from the tomb, the guilt-burdened Jewish leadership began remembering every word that Christ had predicted of His sufferings, death, and resurrection. And from troubled Pilate they begged a guard of soldiers to seal the tomb and watch it so that Christ's disciples could not come and fake a resurrection (Matt. 27:62-66).

Even by comparing the four Gospel accounts we cannot easily put in their exact order and relationship the various steps pertaining to the Christian uniqueness of an empty tomb for its Great Leader, Prophet, Priest, and King. But when the same women who had last left the tomb Friday evening came back, now bringing *their* contribution of spices to do what they could not do because of the Sabbath, they were amazed! Moreover, they are shocked! Soon they are filled with "trembling and astonishment," and "they said nothing to anyone, for they were afraid" (Mark 16:8, R.S.V.). And it was after the young man in a white robe had told them not to be amazed by the empty tomb, for this was what their Lord had told them would happen.

He has risen!

HE IS NOT HERE!

" 'Go, tell his disciples and Peter that he is going before you to Galilee; there you will see him, as he told you' " (verses 6, 7, R.S.V.).

What effort our Lord and His angels had to put forth in order to convince any of His followers that He had risen. Even devoted Mary Magdalene, having seen the empty tomb manned not by soldiers but by angels, tells the "gardener" that she will care for Christ's body if she can just know where it is (John 20:1, 2, 11-15).

John, who claims to believe the testimony of the empty tomb, the folded garments, and who has received messages from the tomb angels, still has problems—"for as yet they did not know the scripture, that he must rise from the dead. Then the disciples went back to their homes" (verses 9, 10, R.S.V.).

HE'S GONE!

That was all they could think of, those disciples of the Lord. But He spent the next several weeks meeting them at different times and places, and under different circumstances to give them every possible evidence that He was not just a stolen body. He was and is a risen Saviour!

In an outstanding article that appeared in the September, 1983, *Ministry,* Dr. Robert M. Johnston, professor of theology at Andrews University Seventh-day Adventist Theological Seminary, examines the question "After Death: Resurrection or Immortality?" He points to four concepts that different cultures have held, the fourth option being that of the resurrection. Concerning it Johnston declares: "This idea is unique and peculiar to Biblical religion; there is no real parallel in paganism."

Johnston evaluates the testimony of the New Testament concerning the resurrection of Christ. It was the heart of apostolic preaching and teaching from Pentecost forward. The "present truth" that occupied the early church was to convince men that Christ had indeed risen from the dead. Thus the sacrifice that He made on the cross entitles Him to raise the believer as He Himself rose.

The New Testament witnesses proclaim the resurrection of Christ as a fact, not an opinion, a theory, or a philosophical proposition. Paul said that at one time there were five hundred witnesses of the resurrected Christ (1 Cor. 15:3-8). And what about their credulity? Some of them were masters of incredulity, like doubting Thomas. And all were risking their very lives to proclaim Christ risen from the dead.

It was a challenge thrown straight into the teeth of the priesthood-dominated Sadducee sect. One of their theological points was the denial of the possibility of resurrection.

The promise of Christ is clear and unequivocal: "Because I live, you will live also" (John 14:19, R.S.V.). "For you have died, and your life is hid with Christ in God. When Christ who is our life appears, then you also will appear with him in glory" (Col. 3:3, 4, R.S.V.).

HE'S GONE: BUT HE'S HERE!

The Lord is not only here, He is right here. Mark's favorite "straightway" will describe the swiftness and power of the Lord's church if she will open her heart and her councils and her ledgers and letters to the movings of the Holy Spirit.

Jesus concentrated His instruction to His disciples about the Holy Spirit's outpouring during the closing hours of His time with them—most probably in the long evening of the Passover Supper in the upper room. But Mark has a little something extra and unique in his account. It, too, may have been given in the same upper room or in connection with the appointment with the eleven to meet in Galilee.

Jesus had appeared to Mary Magdalene, to the two on the way into the country, and several times to the eleven in their hiding place. Having chided them for their unbelief in the light of all the testimony they had received, He made them some promises, perhaps in connection with the pre-Pentecostal breathing of the Spirit upon them (John 20:19-23).

It was not that He had never made similar promises to the disciples before. He had, especially in connection with the missionary journeys on which the Lord had sent them—first the twelve, then the seventy. But this time He repeats the promises briefly on this side of the cross and the empty tomb, and shortly before His ascension to heaven.

It is resurrection power that the Holy Spirit is to bring to the followers of the Lamb of God. The signs and wonders that attend the disciples will confirm their total witness to the Christ. Pentecost is the first recorded manifestation of the gifts of the Spirit. As one would expect, the gifts would match the conditions, circumstances, and challenges faced by the witnesses at the time in which they lived and served.

Pentecost offered a glorious springboard for the Spirit-indited gospel of the cross and the empty tomb. With thousands of worshipers in Jerusalem from all over the Jewish Diaspora with younger generations more familiar with the languages of their adopted countries, the Spirit fulfilled Jesus' promise. The apostles could now speak in languages other than their own. And the miracle of the tongues and the message of the cross and the empty tomb filled the whole festal city.

"He's gone, but He's here" was the theme of Peter's Spirit-filled preaching. It resulted in thousands of converts, who, joining the church eventually returned to their homes at every point of the compass to proclaim with power the saving, transforming good news that had permanently changed their lives. "They will speak in new tongues" (Mark 16:17, R.S.V.) the Saviour declared, and so His followers did. Perhaps that was the newest and most striking (in its time) of the gifts of the Spirit that Paul dealt with in the church at Corinth.

Alongside with the gift of new tongues would continue earlier ones—healing of the sick and casting out of demons from the possessed. These latter two were not one gift. Christ separated them in His instructions and promises. In other words, Mark gives no hint that the sick are also and inevitably demon possessed.

When Jesus earlier had told His disciples that it would be expedient (an advantage, something better) for them that He should go away, they could not possibly have grasped the meaning of His words. They were not yet prepared to accept His swift-coming death as a reality. Why should they grasp His prediction of His permanent departure from them? And even now they are having great difficulty in reconciling His words with their traditional expectations. But the time of tarrying in Jerusalem—seat of Christ's false trials and political murder by both Jewish and Roman leaders—and the bestowal of the promised Holy Spirit changed all that.

Into their minds came flashing the things that He had told them but that the Jewish traditions to which they still clung had made meaningless. As they went out to witness, whether before thousands or in the courts of Jews or Romans, they felt no worry about what they should say. The Holy Spirit prompted them as to what they should speak, and their words had such understanding, conviction, and power that men could scarcely credit either their eyes or their ears. Here were men transformed!

HE'S GONE, but through His followers and in His followers HE'S HERE!

Almost two thousand years have passed into history since the ascension. What is the state of Christ's church today? How is it with Seventh-day Adventists?

Their roots are strong and clearly traceable down to

the great Advent Awakening of the early nineteenth century and on into the development of the Millerite movement on the North American continent. They can even hold up their heads over the great disappointment of October 22, 1844—an experience over which other Christians who still profess to see significance in Biblical apocalyptic chide and somewhat despise Adventists.

But this book should not close without an assurance to Seventh-day Adventists and to their fellow Christian critics that there is no time limitation on the promises of Mark 16:15-20 other than the close of human probation and the second coming of the Lord! In our age of the jet plane, telecommunication, the satellite, the English lingua franca, world famine, and the ever-dangling hydrogen bomb, what spiritual gifts will the church need? The same as in New Testament times? In many areas and respects, why not? Multiple languages and human disease and demon possession still thwart the sweep of the gospel.

We should insist that only the Spirit Himself, who divides the gifts and bestows them on whom He will, can limit the kinds and forms endowed to the church in these last days. The great prerequisite to them could easily be the same as at Pentecost—His followers tarried together while awaiting the heavenly bestowal, and by the grace of Christ they became all one. Perhaps here is a special reason for the devil's efforts to create schism within the Seventh-day Adventist Church. We should pray fervently that we may be one, as the disciples were before the Spirit came in Pentecostal power.

Mark closes his Gospel almost as abruptly as he began it. Others go beyond him with details he does not mention. But after the promise of special gifts to the infant church, Mark's record moves straight to the ascension. It is as bare and spare as it could be. Christ ascends into heaven and sits down at the right hand of God.

HE'S GONE—AGAIN.

But things are happening down here as though He were here! The church went everywhere preaching the gospel of Jesus Christ, while He confirmed or set His seal of approval on their teaching and preaching by the signs or wonders that attended the message (Mark 16:19, 20). And the same must happen again today.

The preparation for Pentecost must be paralleled in the remnant church by Laodiceans as they await the outpouring of latter-rain power with signs *confirming* the present-day message. Note that the signs are not the message, and they are not in themselves proof of truth. The enemy will have similar exhibits—already has had some of them—and flaunts them in our faces. We live in a time of testing. It would be so easy to go out and fall for some counterfeit that looks like Mark 16: 17, 18, but is really Revelation 16:14 in its elemental, precursory form.

Anyway, it is time for the church to bestir herself, to array herself in the garments of the righteousness of Christ, to see obedience as the rightful and testing fruit of saving faith, to put on the whole armor of God, and to seek former-rain cleansing to prepare for latter-rain power (Zech. 10:1; Joel 2:23; James 5:7, 16-18).

And "straightway" we are at the close of Mark's succinct and active Gospel story—perhaps the Gospel according to Peter. And nothing would please either of them more than to know that the remnant of all the remnants of the church has made herself ready for the coming crises and the return of the Son of man in part because of the testimony they have left us of all that Jesus began both to teach and to do from the days of the forerunner until the moment that He ascended up on high.

HE'S GONE—BUT HE'S HERE!

In a moment when we look not for Him, He'll be here again! God prepare us for that day—"straightway"!